MW00781100

The Secret History of Nursery Rhymes

By

Linda Alchin

. . . .

978 0 9567486 1 4
Copyright © Linda Alchin 2013
www.rhymes.org.uk

Edited by Marcus Tidmarsh, Book Design and Layout by Beverley Young.

To

**Our parents who patiently repeated these old, loved Nursery Rhymes
John & Marie Hughes and Richard & Diana Tidmarsh
&
To children who, in their turn, patiently listened to them including
John, Jack & Megan**

. . . .

Linda Alchin is a website author specialising in English history. Her career initially focussed on conventional training techniques to provide adult education. With the advent of the Internet she moved on to distance learning projects. Combining new technology with her love of history she has created a variety of highly successful educational websites which, in turn, have led to the publication of this book. She lives with her family just outside London.

Historical Websites by Linda Alchin:
www.elizabethan-era.org.uk
www.william-shakespeare.info
www.castles.me.uk
www.medieval-life-and-times.info
www.the-tudors.org.uk

Introduction

. . . .

This book uncovers the Secret History of Nursery Rhymes. Many of the history and origins of the humble nursery rhyme are believed to be associated with actual events in history, with references to murder and persecution, betrayal, greed and to tyrants and royalty. Rhymes are usually short and therefore easy to remember, a critical factor during the times when many people were unable to read or write. They were passed verbally from one generation to the next before the invention of the printing press. Reciting old Nursery Rhymes to our children is one of the most pleasurable first steps to developing their language skills and extending their vocabulary. The words were remembered but their secret histories were forgotten.

Although some of the most popular Nursery Rhymes are rooted in English history they are told to children throughout the English-speaking world. Old English Nursery Rhymes were taken to America with the settlers from England. They were then spread across Commonwealth countries including Canada, Australia and New Zealand.

Political satire was cleverly disguised in the wording of some, seemingly innocent, nursery rhymes. These were used as safe vehicles to parody unpopular political, royal and historical events of the day. By this simple process subversive messages of discontent were spread in times when words of dissent, or the direct criticism of powerful people, would often have been punishable by torture or death.

Some interpretations of the rhymes are controversial; you may agree with some ideas and disagree with others! Are they Truth or Fallacy? Difficult to decide considering much of our 'accepted' history is often based on pure conjecture. History is also biased! This view is perfectly illustrated in the words of Winston Churchill who once said "History will be kind to me for I intend to write it".

Another Winston also comes to mind when considering the subject of truth. In the George Orwell novel, Nineteen Eighty-Four (1984) the nursery rhyme 'Oranges and Lemons' is only partially remembered by the principal character, Winston Smith. Various characters contribute snippets of the rhyme until the verse is completed. But it is lost forever when the final few people who remember it all die. Thankfully, we do not yet live in the world described in Orwell's Nineteen Eighty-Four and there is no Big Brother to prevent the eradication of our culture and the publication of books such as this...

CONTENTS

History of Rhymes

Popular Rhymes

. . . .

People Rhymes

. . . .

Useful, Historic & Weather Lore Rhymes

. . . .

Epic Tales

Chapbooks

The Nursery Rhyme began to be printed in England as early as 1570, up to this point rhymes that had been passed to different generations verbally, then started to be passed on via the written form. Printing allowed the production of books and cheap pamphlets, or Chapbooks. A chapbook is "a small book or pamphlet containing 24 pages or less without a hard cover. It contains poems, ballads, stories, or religious tracts, and they were usually anonymous and undated. The popularity of Chapbooks increased during the 1600's, 1700's and 1800's but only a few of the early copies have survived. More people during this time were learning to read but the chapbooks were very popular with illiterate majority as they contained pictures of crude wood engravings. The Chapbook was a Medieval equivalent of a Child's comic - documenting funny rhymes and folklore. The contents were committed from memory which accounts for some variations in the lyrics and words of some Nursery Rhymes. The content and material expanded in the 1700's to include children's stories like Robinson Crusoe and various versions of Perrault's Fairy Tales.

Southwark Fair, in London

The Chapmen
Chapbooks were sold by Chapmen or peddlers who sold, amongst other wares, the popular penny Chapbooks at local fairs. The Chapmen sold various wares that were easy to transport from one village or fair to the next and they attracted attention by dancing and singing the old familiar Rhymes. The word 'Chap' originates in Middle English, from the Old English 'capman' meaning 'trade' add this to the word 'cheap' to provide a full definition of a Chapman. These old Chap books have given us most of our old Nursery Rhymes. English Ballads, Folklore and old legends were also documented in the books and sung by wandering minstrels which helped to continue the spread of the old Nursery Rhymes and Legends.

The Chapbook Printers and Publishers
The leading chapbook printers in 1780 included John Marshall who published, printed and sold chapbooks in the Aldermary Churchyard which was situated next to the Church of St Mary Aldermary in Bow Lane, London. It is also of interest to note that Newbery Publishing House, who published "Mother Goose's Melody" or "Sonnets for the Cradle", was also set up in a similar location in St. Paul's churchyard.

Mother Goose Publications

· · · · · · · · · · · · · · · · ·

The first known publication of a collection of Nursery Rhymes was in 1744 and the first confirmed collection of Nursery Rhymes using the term "Mother Goose" was published in 1780, although a collection of stories called "Mother Goose's Tales" was published in 1729. The Mother Goose term caught the imagination of printers, publishers and the general public. Invariably the illustrations accompanying the publications depicted Mother Goose as an old crone, or a witch. Various claims have been made claiming ownership of the term 'Mother Goose', our search for the origins have established the following information.

The French Connection

1650 - The earliest known written reference, which uses the term 'Mother Goose' in relation to a collection of stories, was in a monthly periodical by the French critic Jean Loret (1610 - 1665) in his 1650 "La Muse Historique" which contains the line, "Comme un conte de la Mére Oye" which translates into "Like a Mother Goose story".

1697 - A collection of eight famous folk tales which included Sleeping Beauty, Little Red Riding Hood and Cinderella was published in 1697 by a French man called Charles Perrault. The book was called "Histories and Tales of Long Ago, with Morals" and the frontispiece (title page) contained the words "Contes de ma mère l'Oye" or "Tales of Mother Goose" but contained none of the rhymes we associate with Mother Goose, most of which have obvious English origins. The illustration on the frontispiece depicted an old witch-like woman spinning and telling stories.

The English Theory

1729 - Perrault's tales were translated into English in 1729 by Robert Samber and published in the same year. The words on the frontispiece were "Mother Goose's Tales".

1744 - The earliest known collection of Nursery Rhymes called "Tommy Thumb's Song Book" was published in London by Mary Cooper.

1744 - A bookseller and publisher called John Newbery (1713-1767) set up his business in St. Paul's churchyard. He published his first children's book in the same year called "The Little Pretty Pocket Book" which was dedicated to "the Parents, Guardians and Nurses in Great Britain and Ireland". It was an instant hit and it became apparent to John Newbery that his firm could make substantial profits by publishing children's tales and rhymes. They established Children's literature as an important branch of the publishing business, his most successful publication was "Little Goody Two Shoes" which was published in 1766.

1780 - Thomas Carnan, the stepson of John Newbery, became the owner of the Newbery Publishing House following Newbery's death in 1767. Thomas Carnan entered the title "Mother Goose's Melody" or "Sonnets for the Cradle" at the London Stationer's Hall. It was described as a compilation of traditional English nonsense songs and rhymes. It contained fifty-two rhymes each with its own black and white illustration which was given additional marketing credibility by the inclusion of sixteen verses from Shakespeare.

The American Story
Within a few years there were several pirated editions of the Newbery Mother Goose published in America, one with the picture of a sharp-nosed old crone addressing two children as follows:

"Fudge! I tell you that all their batterings can't deface my beauties, nor their wise pratlings my wiser prattlings; and all imitators of my refreshing songs might as well try to write a new Billy Shakespeare as another Mother Goose! We two great poets were born together, and we shall go out of the world together. No, No, my melodies will never die, While nurses sing, or babies cry."

1786 - Isaiah Thomas published the first authorised American edition of "Mother Goose's Melody".

1860 - It was claimed in 1860 that a collection of Mother Goose children's nursery rhymes had been published in Boston by Thomas Fleet in 1719 under the title "Songs of the Nursery" or "Mother Goose's Melodies for Children". On the title page was the picture of a goose with a very long neck and a mouth wide open, and below this, "Printed by T. Fleet, at his Printing House in Pudding Lane, 1719. Price, two coppers." Thomas Fleet was born in England in 1685 and moved to America in 1712 - he died in Boston, Massachusetts in 1758. He married Elizabeth Goose (written also as Vergoose and Vertigoose), the daughter of a wealthy Bostonian on 8th June 1715 and it is claimed that he used her name to originate the term Mother Goose. This claim has been investigated but there is no evidence to support it. There is not a single known copy of any such book in existence or indeed any documented record relating to a book with this title prior to the date the claim was made.

1878 - "Mother Goose in White" was published.

1879 - "The Old Fashioned Mother Goose Melodies" were published.

1916 - McNally & Company re published the collection of "Mother Goose Rhymes" as "The Real Mother Goose".

1928 - "Mother Goose Nursery Rhymes" arranged by Logan Marshall was published in Chicago with illustrations by Julia Gree.

Old Mother Goose

Old Mother Goose
When she wanted to wander
Would fly through the air
On a very fine gander.

Mother Goose had a house;
It stood in the wood
Where an owl at the door
As sentinel stood.

. . . .

Cackle, Cackle, Mother Goose

Cackle, cackle, Mother Goose,
Have you any feathers loose?
Truly have I, pretty fellow,
Half enough to fill a pillow.
Here are quills, take one or two,
And down to make a bed for you.

Why Mother Goose?

The words of these original Old Mother Goose Nursery Rhymes can be interpreted to find a darker meaning to the identity of Mother Goose. The term Mother Goose probably originates from the 1600's - the time of the great witch hunts and comparisons can be made between the Mother Goose and popular conception of a witch during this era:

- Witches were able to fly - the broomstick has been replaced by a goose, hence the name Mother Goose.
- A witch was often portrayed as an old crone, with no man to defend her against accusations of witchcraft.
- Witches are closely associated with living alone - in house in the wood.

Witches, Familiars and Nursery Rhymes

Witches were known to a have 'familiars' - an evil spirit, in animal form, which was used by the witch to perform evil deeds and cast malevolent spells. 'Familiars' were most often cats but could also be other small animals including frogs, pigs, ravens, goats, wolves, geese, crows, bats, mice and owls, just like the modern wizard Harry Potter whose owl is called Hedwig.

People were obsessed with witches during the 16th and 17th centuries when there was limited understanding of the cause of devastating events, such as storms, drought and disease. The disasters were believed to be brought about by supernatural forces which resulted in scapegoats (witches) being blamed. A book called the 'Malleus Maleficarum' was published in 1486 as guide used for the torture and persecution of witches - a best selling book of those times, only being out-sold by the Bible.

Witchcraft was outlawed in England in 1563 and a Witchcraft Act was passed in 1604. The witchcraft hysteria grew and eventually led to the Parliamentary appointment of Matthew Hopkins as Witchfinder General in 1644. His task was to seek out witches he was vigorous in his work as he was said to have been paid twenty shillings for each witch he condemned. During his interrogations he was guided by books like the 'Malleus Maleficarum' which stated that an animal familiar "always works with the witch in everything".

Many Nursery Rhymes originated in the 16th and 17th centuries and the children of these times would have been familiar (sorry about the pun!) with stories of witches and witchcraft.

Just look at the image of Mother Goose who is portrayed as a witch with her familiar (the goose). Is it therefore just a coincidence that so many of the Nursery rhymes of the periods featured so many small animals?

Three Blind Mice

Popular Rhymes

. . . .

An Apple a Day
Baa Baa Black Sheep
Boys and Girls Come Out to Play
Christmas is Coming
Cry Baby Bunting
Diddle Diddle Dumpling
Ding Dong Bell
For Want of a Nail
Goosey Goosey Gander
Hark Hark the Dogs do Bark
Hey Diddle Diddle
Hickory Dickory Dock
Hot Cross Buns
Humpty Dumpty
Hush a Bye Baby
I Had a Little Nut Tree
Ladybug Ladybug (Ladybird Ladybird)
Pat a Cake Pat a Cake
Pease Pudding Hot
Pop goes the Weasel
Pussycat Pussycat
Rain Rain go Away
Ride a Cock Horse to Banbury Cross
Ring Around the Rosy (Ring a Ring of Roses)
Sing a Song of Sixpence
There was a Crooked Man
There was an Old Woman
Three Blind Mice

An Apple a Day

· · · · · · · · · · · · · · · · ·

An apple a day keeps the doctor away
Apple in the morning - Doctor's warning
Roast apple at night - Starves the doctor outright
Eat an apple going to bed - Knock the doctor on the head
Three each day, seven days a week - Ruddy apple, ruddy cheek.

The author of the poem An Apple a Day is unknown
it was first cited in print in 1866.

· · · · · · · · · · · · · · · · ·

The sentiment expressed in this poem is one to encourage the child to eat healthily and wisely. Although perhaps 'Doctor' could be substituted with 'Dentist' in a modern day version of this rhyme. What's the truth behind the saying? A medium sized apple has only 75 calories, contains calcium and vitamins A, B1, B2, C and E, cholesterol free and is beneficial for all age groups.

Apples were brought to North America with colonists in the 17th century. Prior to this time only wild apples or crab apples were found in America. The first apple orchard was cultivated in 1623 by William Blackstone on Beacon Hill in Boston.

Medieval Physicians were expected to care for people with the deadly Bubonic Plague, which explains the bizarre clothing they wore. Take a close look at what the Physician is wearing in the picture. All of his body is completely covered from head to foot, even his face. The bizarre mask features a long beak which was filled with bergamot oil, this gruesome mask would have acted as some protection against contracting diseases through breathing the same air as the patient. Stout boots and gloves covered his hands and feet and long dark robes with pointed hoods, were also worn as a form of protection. They completed their clothing by wearing amulets of dried blood and ground-up toads which were worn around their waists. Although many of these ideas might sound pointless today they would have been extremely effective in preventing the Physician from being bitten by fleas which, although unknown at the time, actually spread the Bubonic Plague.

Baa Baa Black Sheep

. . . .

Baa baa black sheep, have you any
wool?
Yes sir, yes sir, three bags full,
One for the master, one for the dame,
And one for the little boy
who lives down the lane.

The earliest publication date is 1744. The music was
first published in the early nineteenth century.

. . . .

The History and Origins of Baa Baa Black Sheep
The wool industry was critical to England's economy from the Middle
Ages until the nineteenth century so it is therefore not surprising that it
is celebrated in the Baa Baa Black Sheep Nursery Rhyme. A historical
connection for this rhyme has been suggested - a political satire said to refer
to the Plantagenet King Edward I (the Master) and the export tax imposed
in Britain in 1275 in which the English Customs Statute authorised the
king to collect a tax on all exports of wool in every port in the country.

Further research indicates another possible connection of this Nursery rhyme
to English history relating to King Edward II (1307-1327). The best wool in
Europe was produced in England but the cloth workers from Flanders, Bruges
and Lille were better skilled in the complex finishing trades such as dying
and fulling (cleansing, shrinking, and thickening the cloth). King Edward II
encouraged Flemmish weavers and cloth dyers to improve the quality of the final
English products.

2006 - The Nursery Rhyme War
In 2006 the words to this old rhyme were changed, by some English nurseries,
to Baa Baa, Rainbow Sheep in order to meet requirements of policies for Equal
Opportunities. There were concerns that it might be deemed offensive to refer
to a sheep as "black" so this word was replaced with "rainbow". The measure
sparked considerable public debate objecting to the Big Brother attitude of
officials who were forcing compliance by rewriting children's ditties to make
them more socially acceptable and politically correct.

Boys and Girls Come Out to Play

. . . .

Boys and girls come out to play,
The moon does shine as bright as day;
Come with a hoop, and come with a call,
Come with a good will or not at all.
Loose your supper, and loose your sleep,
Come to your playfellows in the street;
Up the ladder and down the wall.
A halfpenny loaf will serve us all.
But when the loaf is gone, what will you do?
Those who would eat must work – 'tis true.

First published in 1708.

. . . .

The Nursery Rhyme, Boys and Girls Come Out to Play refers to the time when most children had to work "Those who would eat must work" and there was little time for play. Playtime was in the evening, after the day's work "The moon does shine as bright as day" and "Loose your supper, and loose your sleep". Up to the time of the industrial revolution children would help their parents on the land, only the children of wealthy parents would attend school, so this rhyme referred to the period in history where children did not have time to play.

Child Labour
The 19th century brought the age of the indus-trial revolution and factories. Many children, especially workhouse children, worked for over 16 hours a day under atrocious conditions in factories, mills and mines. Children of small stature were found particularly useful in chimney sweeping. Children began work at the age of five and generally died before they were 25 due to the terrible working conditions they had endured.

Christmas is Coming

. . . .

Christmas is coming, the geese are getting fat
Please to put a penny in the old man's hat;
If you haven't got a penny, a ha'penny will do,
If you haven't got a ha'penny then God bless you!

. . . .

The charitable lyrics of Christmas is Coming associates the Christmas festivity of eating geese with a reminder that the festive period is where each should give to charity according to their means... even if all they could give was their blessing (If you haven't got a penny...)

History of the Penny
The history of the English penny is not commonly known but is a vital part of English history and heritage. The first documented reference to the penny is dated 790 AD when the first British penny was minted in silver. The design of the penny frequently changed depicting the images of various rulers. The first Anglo-Saxon pennies depicted a cross on the reverse of the coin as a symbol of

Christianity. These crosses were used as guidelines to cut the penny into halves and quarters - "cut coinage". The halfpenny (worth half the value of a penny) and farthing (worth a quarter, or a fourth, of the value of a penny) were then minted. The word farthing was derived from 'fourthing'. The penny changed from silver to copper in 1797 (hence the colloquialism 'coppers') then changed to bronze in 1860 and copper plated steel in 1992. The Nursery Rhyme Christmas is Coming can claim to be instrumental in maintaining our heritage in relation to the coinage of both the UK and the USA which also used the humble penny.

Cry Baby Bunting

. . . .

Cry Baby Bunting
Daddy's gone a-hunting
Gone to fetch a rabbit skin
To wrap the Baby Bunting in
Cry Baby Bunting.

. . . .

The lyrics of the poem Cry Baby Bunting were not intended to be important - it was the sound of the soothing music to accompany it. The rhyme would be sung softly to a young child as a lullaby. Perhaps to explain the disappearance of Father to a crying child. The earliest traceable publication is 1784, there is however a version of this lullaby which clearly has American roots with the reference to the pumpkin.

Alternative Lyrics

Bye, Baby Bumpkin
Where is Tony Lumpkin?*
My lady is on her death-bed,
For eating half a pumpkin.

* Tony Lumpkin is a fictional comedy character who first appeared in Oliver Goldsmith's play, She Stoops to Conquer.

18

Diddle Diddle Dumpling

. . . .

Diddle, Diddle, Dumpling, my son John,
Went to bed with his trousers on;
One shoe off, and one shoe on,
Diddle, Diddle, Dumpling, my son John!

. . . .

No origins in history can be found for Diddle Diddle Dumpling - it is merely a nonsense rhyme probably made popular and handed down from generation to generation owing to the popularity of the name John. It is an interesting fact that this is the only old rhyme that uses the name John - all of the older poems use the colloquialism for John i.e. Jack.

The Story of a Famous John - John of Gaunt

A Plantagenet prince, the rich and powerful John of Gaunt (1340 - 1399). His liaison with a commoner called Katherine Swynford produced four illegitimate children who were given the name Beaufort (He married Katherine in 1396 and their children, by this time adults, were legitimised). Their son John was the Great-Great Grandfather of King Henry VIII of England

Ding Dong Bell

· · · · · · · · · · · · · · · · ·

Ding Dong Bell
Pussy's in the well
Who put her in?
Little Johnny Flynn
Who pulled her out?
Little Tommy Stout
What a naughty boy was that
Try to drown poor Pussycat,
Who ne'er did any harm
But killed all the mice
In the Farmer's barn!

· · · · · · · · · · · · · · · · ·

The origins of this nursery rhyme date back to the 16th century and the era of Shakespeare who used the phrase Ding Dong Bell in several plays. The original lyrics actually ended with the cat being left to drown! These words were modified and the cat was saved by Little Tommy Stout to encourage children to understand that it was unacceptable and cruel to harm any animal 'who ne'er did any harm'. The latter version taught morality at an early age. Ding Dong Bell, also introduces a child to onomatopoeia (a word that sounds like its meaning) In this nursery rhyme the lyrics and words Ding Dong when pronounced convey the actual sounds.

The Shakespeare Connection
The phrase Ding Dong Bell was used by William Shakespeare - but given the original drafts of Shakespeare plays were in Quarto text and the majority were not published until 1623 in the First Folio (7 years after his death) could the phrase actually be the writer's original instructions for sound effects?

The Tempest, Act I, Scene II:
"Sea nymphs hourly ring his knell: Hark! Now I hear them - Ding, dong, bell."

The Merchant of Venice, Act III, Scene II:
"Let us all ring fancy's bell; I'll begin it - Ding, dong, bell."

For Want of a Nail

· · · · · · · · · · · · · · · · ·

For want of a nail the shoe was lost.
For want of a shoe the horse was lost.
For want of a horse the rider was lost.
For want of a rider the battle was lost.
For want of a battle the kingdom was lost.
And all for the want of a horseshoe nail.

The earliest known written version of the rhyme is in John Gower's
Confesio Amantis dated approximately 1390.

· · · · · · · · · · · · · · · · ·

A clever set of lyrics that encourage children to apply logical progression to the consequences of their actions. For Want of a Nail is often used to gently chastise a child whilst explaining the possible events that may follow a thoughtless act.

The History of Obligatory Archery Practise
The references to horses, riders, kingdoms and battles indicate the English origins of the rhyme. One of the English Kings did not leave anything to chance, in 1363 to ensure the continued safety of the realm, King Edward III commanded the obligatory practice of archery on Sundays and holidays.

"For Want of a Nail" American usage
Benjamin Franklin included a version of the rhyme in his Poor Richard's Almanac when America and England were on opposite sides.

During World War II, this verse was framed and hung on the wall of the Anglo-American Supply Headquarters in London, England.

Edward III counting the
dead on the battlefield

Goosey Goosey Gander

. . . .

Goosey Goosey Gander where shall I wander,
Upstairs, downstairs and in my lady's chamber
There I met an old man who wouldn't say his prayers,
I took him by the left leg and threw him down the stairs.

. . . .

Caught in the Act -
Religious Intolerance, Zealous Protestants & Secret Priest Holes

Goosey, Goosey Gander is a rhyme with historical undertones - an attention grabber for a nursery rhyme which uses alliteration in the lyrics designed to intrigue any child. The lady's chamber was a room that a high born lady would have for her personal needs (also referred to as a solar). The origins are believed to date back to the 16th century and refer to necessity for Catholic priests to hide in Priest Holes (very small secret rooms once found in many great houses in England) to avoid persecution from zealous Protestants who were totally against the old Catholic religion. If caught both the priest and members of any family found harbouring them were executed. The moral in Goosey Goosey Gander's lyrics imply that something unpleasant would surely happen to anyone failing to say their prayers correctly - meaning the Protestant Prayers, said in English as opposed to Catholic prayers which were said in Latin.

GOOSEY GOOSEY GANDER

Hark Hark the Dogs do Bark

. . . .

Hark hark the dogs do bark
The beggars are coming to town
Some in rags and some in jags*
And one in a velvet gown.

. . . .

A Sinister Tale

During Medieval times wandering minstrels or troubadours went from city to town singing their songs. Messages of dissent to the common people were often found in secret meanings to the words of their ballads. In this way the propaganda of the day was safely passed from one community to another. These secret messages could lead to plots and uprisings against the royalty, clergy and politicians of the day. In Saxon England, professional storytellers, called 'scops' would also travel around the country telling stories for their living. A theory in relation to its origins refers to the Dissolution of the Monasteries (1536 - 1540) when England broke from the Catholic religion and the Church of England was established. This act was perpetrated by King Henry VIII and his chief minister Thomas Cromwell. Their objective was to loot the monasteries and seize the monastic lands (which they promptly sold) thus increasing the wealth in the coffers of England. Hundreds of monks and nuns were made homeless, the main source of charity for the old and infirm was eliminated which resulted in a vast increase in the number of beggars. The Tudor and Elizabethan governments made begging a crime and they would be beaten until they reached the stones that marked the town parish boundary. During outbreaks of the Bubonic Plague any strangers or beggars were looked upon with horror. Dogs barking alerted the townspeople to strangers in their area, hence the words "Hark, hark the dogs do bark ..."

King Henry VIII who broke with the Catholic Church and dissolved the English Monasteries

Hey Diddle Diddle

. . . .

Hey diddle diddle, the cat and the fiddle,
The cow jumped over the moon.
The little dog laughed to see such fun
And the dish ran away with the spoon.

The first known date of publication was in Mother Goose's Melody c1765.

. . . .

Imaginative words to Hey Diddle Diddle

This fantasy rhyme is designed to delight children with impossible images such as the "Cow jumped over the Moon". Walt Disney's team of animators use this type of imagery in animated films to great effect. The term Hey Diddle Diddle can be found in the works of Shakespeare and was a colloquialism used in much the same vein as "Hey Nonny No" which can be found in traditional English folk ballads. The original title was High Diddle Diddle but this has been altered to Hey Diddle Diddle over the years with changes to the English language.

Portrait of William Shakespeare

Hickory Dickory Dock

. . . .

Hickory Dickory Dock
The mouse ran up the clock
The clock struck one
The mouse ran down
Hickory dickory dock.

The earliest publication was in Tommy Thumb's Pretty Song Book,
London 1744.

. . . .

Action Rhyme reflected in the words of Hickory Dickory Dock
A nonsense poem which uses alliteration where children mimic the sound of
a clock chiming at the relevant point in the song, it is also intended to introduce
children to the fundamentals of telling the time. Investigation into the meanings
of the words used lead us to believe that it has its origins in America.

The Origins of Hickory
Hickory is a derived from the North American Indian word Pawcohiccora which
is an oily milk-like liquor that is pressed from pounded hickory nuts. The word
Pohickory was contained in a list of Virginia trees published in 1653, the word
was subsequently shortened to hickory.

The Origins of Dock
Dock is a species of plant which has the Latin name of Rumex crispus. A
well-known weed which has a long taproot making it difficult to exterminate.
The Dock plant can be used as an astringent or tonic and many of us would
have experienced the healing properties of the Dock leaf after being stung by a
stinging nettle.

Hot Cross Buns

Hot cross buns! Hot cross buns!
One a penny two a penny - Hot cross buns
If you have no daughters, give them to your sons
One a penny two a penny - Hot cross buns!

First published in Christmas Box, in London c1798.

. . . .

Religious meaning of Hot Cross Buns

Hot cross buns are small, spicy fruit bread buns decorated with a white cross, generally they are served with a butter spread. Traditionally they were hawked by street sellers to the cry of "Hot cross buns!" Around the nineteenth century. This particular way of selling wares is demonstrated in the movie 'Oliver' based on the novel Oliver Twist by Charles Dickens. Hot Cross Buns are generally sold at Easter to celebrate the religious significance of the resurrection of Jesus Christ following his death on the cross during the Easter Christian festival. The crucifixion, being symbolised on the bun with the cross, although now eaten throughout the Easter holidays Hot Cross Buns were originally only eaten on Good Friday and were symbolic of partaking Holy Bread or Communion - the body of Christ at this special Christian time.

Mr. Bumble from Dickens Oliver Twist.

Humpty Dumpty

· · · · · · · · · · · · · · · · ·

Humpty Dumpty sat on a wall,
Humpty Dumpty had a great fall.
All the King's horses, And all the King's men
Couldn't put Humpty together again!

Earliest traceable publication 1810.

· · · · · · · · · · · · · · · · ·

Humpty Dumpty was a colloquial term used in fifteenth century England describing someone who was obese. This has given rise to various, but inaccurate, theories surrounding the identity of him. The image of Humpty Dumpty was made famous by the illustrations included in the 'Alice Through The Looking Glass' novel by Lewis Carroll. However, it was not the person pilloried in the famous rhyme. Humpty Dumpty was in fact believed to be a large cannon which was used during the English Civil War (1642 - 1649) in the Siege of Colchester (13 Jun 1648 - 27 Aug 1648). Colchester was strongly fortified by the Royalists, (Cavaliers) and was laid to siege by the Parliamentarians (Roundheads). In 1648 the town of Colchester had a castle and several churches, which were protected by a surrounding city wall. Standing immediately adjacent the city wall was St Mary's Church. A huge cannon, commonly referred to as Humpty Dumpty was strategically placed on the wall next to St Mary's Church. The historical events detailing the siege of Colchester are well documented - references to the cannon (Humpty Dumpty) are as follows:

June 15th 1648 - St Mary's Church is fortified and a large cannon is placed on the roof which was fired by 'One-Eyed Jack Thompson'.

July 14th / July 15th 1648 - The Royalist fort within the walls at St Mary's church is blown to pieces and their main cannon battery (Humpty Dumpty) is destroyed.

August 28th 1648 - The Royalists lay down their arms, open the gates of Colchester and surrender to the Parliamentarians.

A shot from a Parliamentary cannon succeeded in damaging the wall beneath Humpty Dumpty which caused the cannon to tumble to the ground. The Royalists or Cavaliers, 'all the King's men' attempted to raise Humpty Dumpty on

to another part of the wall. However, because the cannon, was so heavy that 'All the King's horses and all the King's men couldn't put Humpty together again.' This had a drastic consequence for the Royalists as the strategically important town of Colchester fell to the Parliamentarians after a siege lasting eleven weeks.

* A Roundhead (Parliamentarian) was so called from the close-cropped hair of the Puritans.

* The word Cavalier is derived from the French word Chevalier meaning a military man serving on horseback - a knight. Cheval being french for a horse.

Hush a Bye Baby

Hush a bye baby, on the tree top,
When the wind blows the cradle will rock;
When the bow breaks, the cradle will fall,
And down will come baby, cradle and all.

First published in 1765.

Is "Hush a Bye Baby" a Nursery Rhyme or lullaby?

Hush a Bye Baby is said to have originated in America. It was apparently the practice of some Native Americans to place a baby in the branches of a tree allowing the wind to gently rock the child to sleep as in Hush a Bye Baby on the Treetop. The meaning to the words of the rhyme seem to match this explanation. The words to the song are intended to soothe a child to sleep so the song can therefore be correctly described as both a nursery rhyme and a lullaby. Another version of the rhyme was published in Songs for Nursery (1805) which contained the wording "Rock-a-bye, Baby, Thy Cradle is Green, Father's a Nobleman, Mother's a Green". The two versions were combined together over time and the words 'Hush a Bye Baby' was replaced with 'Rock a Bye Baby'.

I Had a Little Nut Tree

. . . .

I had a little nut tree,
Nothing would it bear
But a silver nutmeg,
And a golden pear;
The King of Spain's daughter
Came to visit me,
And all for the sake
Of my little nut tree.

First Published in Newest Christmas Box London in 1797.

. . . .

The characters in the rhyme are believed to refer to the visit of the Royal House of Spain to King Henry VII's English court in 1506. The 'King of Spain's daughter' refers to the daughter of King Ferdinand and Queen Isabella of Spain. There were two daughters, Princess Juana and her sister Katherine of Aragon. The princess in the nursery rhyme is probably Katherine of Aragon who was betrothed to Prince Arthur, the heir to the throne of England. Arthur died and Katherine eventually married King Henry VIII. Katherine of Aragon was the first of Henry's six wives and was discarded by the King to make way for Anne Boleyn. Queen Katherine was much loved by the British people who hated her replacement.

The fate of the wives of King Henry VIII (Katherine of Aragon, Anne Boleyn, Jane Seymour, Anne of Cleves, Catherine Howard and Katherine Parr, respectively) are remembered by this little poem:

Divorced, beheaded, died.
Divorced, beheaded, survived.

Katherine of Aragon

Ladybug Ladybug (Ladybird Ladybird)

. . . .

Ladybug ladybug fly away home,
Your house in on fire and your children are gone,
All except one and that's little Ann,
For she crept under the frying pan.

The first publication date was 1865 and the word ladybird was used as opposed to ladybug. There has been some speculation that this Nursery Rhyme originates from the time of the Great Fire of London in 1666.

. . . .

Traditional Nursery Rhyme
"Ladybug, Ladybug" is chanted by children when a ladybug insect lands on their person. If the ladybug doesn't fly away of its own accord the child would gently blow it away chanting "Ladybug Ladybug fly away home". This insect is found every summer in the gardens of Britain they are referred to as 'ladybirds'.

Ladybird History Connection - Gunpowder Plot Conspirators?
Farmers knew of the ladybird's value in reducing the level of pests in their crops and it was traditional for them to cry out the rhyme before they burnt their fields following harvests (this reduced the level of insects and pests) in deference to the helpful ladybird.

The English word ladybird is a derivative of the Catholic term " Our Lady". The tradition of calling this rhyme was believed to have been used as a seemingly innocent warning cry to Catholic (recusants) who refused to attend Protestant services as required by the Act of Uniformity (1559 & 1662). This law forbade priests to say Mass and forbade communicants to attend it. Consequently Mass was held secretly in the open fields. Laymen were subject to jail and heavy fines and priests to execution. Many priests were executed by the terrible death of being burnt alive at the stake or, even worse, being hung, drawn and quartered. The most famous English recusants were Guy Fawkes and the Gunpowder Plot Conspirators.

The American Version of the Lyrics
It is possible that the word Ladybird was exchanged for Ladybug, in the American version of the nursery rhyme, due the word association with Firebug meaning an arsonist or pyromaniac.

LADYBIRD LADYBIRD

Pat a Cake Pat a Cake

· · · · · · · · · · · · · · · · · · ·

Pat a cake, Pat a cake, baker's man
Bake me a cake as fast as you can;
Pat it and prick it and mark it with 'B',
And put it in the oven for Baby and Me.

The earliest traceable publication was in 1698.

· · · · · · · · · · · · · · · · ·

The origins of this poem are unknown, but the tradition of decorating cakes with the name or initial of a child is still adhered to today. The song Pat a Cake is always accompanied by a clapping game - much loved by children everywhere. The actions which accompany Pat a Cake probably account for the ritual of passing this particular song from one generation to the next.

Historical Note: The Bakers of London

The Great Fire of London of 1666 started in a baker's shop, in Pudding Lane and ravaged the City. Bakeries were always considered to be a huge fire risk to the timber built buildings of London. One positive thing about the Great Fire was that it helped to cleanse the city of the Plague.

Pease Pudding Hot

· · · · · · · · · · · · · · · · ·

Pease pudding hot, Pease pudding cold,
Pease pudding in the pot - nine days old.
Some like it hot, some like it cold,
Some like it in the pot - nine days old.

The first publication of this rhyme was in
John Newbery's Mother Goose's Melody c. 1760.

· · · · · · · · · · · · · · · · ·

The pease pudding hot referred to in the words of this poem is a dish which is
still enjoyed in Britain today. It is a smooth, thick sauce, (referred to as a pudding
in the rhyme for the sake of alliteration) which has a dark yellow colour. Pease
pudding is a hot dish made from dried peas - it can be re-heated as often as
required (Pease pudding in the pot - nine days old). Pease pudding is traditionally
served hot with boiled bacon or with a form of sausage called a saveloy.

Pop goes the Weasel

· · · · · · · · · · · · · · · ·

Half a pound of tuppenny rice, Half a pound of treacle.
That's the way the money goes, Pop! goes the weasel.
Up and down the City road, In and out the Eagle,
That's the way the money goes, Pop! goes the weasel.

First published in 1855.

· · · · · · · · · · · · · · · ·

This nursery rhyme sounds quite incomprehensible in this day and age. The origins are believed to date back to the 1700's and some translation is in order.

Pop and Weasel?

These words are derived from Cockney Rhyming Slang which originated in London. Cockneys were a close community and had a suspicion of strangers and a dislike of the Police (they still do!). Cockneys developed a language of their own based roughly on a rhyming slang - it was difficult for strangers to understand as invariably the second noun would always be dropped. Apples and Pears (meaning stairs) would be abbreviated to just 'apples', for instance, "watch your step on the apples". To 'Pop' is the slang word for 'Pawn'. Weasel is derived from 'weasel and stoat' meaning coat. It was traditional for even poor people to own a suit, which they wore as their Sunday best. When times were hard they would pawn their suit, or coat, on a Monday and claim it back before Sunday. Hence the term " Pop goes the Weasel".

In and out the Eagle?

The Eagle refers to 'The Eagle Tavern' a pub which is located on the corner of City Road and Shepherdess Walk in Hackney, North London. The Eagle was an old pub which was re-built as a music hall in 1825. Charles Dickens (1812-1870) was known to frequent the Music Hall. It was purchased by the Salvation Army in 1883 (they were totally opposed to drinking and Music Halls). The hall was later demolished and was rebuilt as a public house in 1901.

Alternative Lyrics

"A penny for a spool of thread, a penny for a needle" - this version has led to a 'weasel' being interpreted as a shuttle or bobbin, as used by silk weavers, being pawned in a similar way as the suits or jackets owned by the Cockneys.

Pussycat Pussycat

. . . .

"Pussycat pussycat, where have you been?"
"I've been up to London to visit the Queen."
"Pussycat pussycat, what did you there?"
"I frightened a little mouse under a chair"
"MEOWW!"

First published in Songs for the Nursery, printed in London in 1805.

. . . .

The origins of the nursery rhyme Pussycat Pussycat

This rhyme is believed to date back to the history of 16th century Tudor England. One of the waiting ladies of Queen Elizabeth I had an old cat which roamed throughout Windsor Castle. On one particular occasion the cat ran beneath the throne where its tail brushed against the Queen's foot, startling her. Luckily 'Good Queen Bess' had a sense of humour and decreed that the cat could wander about the throne room, on condition it kept it free of mice!

Windsor Castle

Rain Rain Go Away

Rain rain go away,
Come again another day.
Little Johnny wants to play;
Rain, rain, go to Spain,
Never show your face again!

The origin of the words to Rain Rain Go Away are said to date back to the reign of Queen Elizabeth I (1533-1603), one of the English Tudor monarchs. During this period of English history there was constant rivalry between Spain and England culminating in the launch of the Spanish Armada in 1588.

The Spanish Armada, led by Duke of Medina Sedonia, consisted of over 130 Spanish galleons and ships, which were sent to invade England. The English fleet, under Admiral Lord Howard, totalled 34 small Navy vessels and 163 armed merchant ships, but they defeated the great Spanish Armada. Only 65 Spanish galleons and just 10,000 men returned to Spain. The attempt failed, not only because of the swift nature of the smaller English ships but also by the stormy weather which scattered the Armada fleet. Hence the origin of Rain Rain Go Away.

Ride a Cock Horse to Banbury Cross

. . . .

Ride a cock horse to Banbury Cross
To see a fine lady upon a white horse
With rings on her fingers and bells on her toes
She shall have music wherever she goes

First published in Tommy Thumb's Pretty Song Book,

printed in London c.1744.

. . . .

The words of Banbury Cross are often attributed to Queen Elizabeth I of England (the fine lady) who travelled to Banbury to see a huge stone cross which had just been erected. The words "With rings on her fingers" obviously relates to the fine jewellery which would be worn by a Queen, 'And bells on her toes' refer to the fashion of attaching bells to the end of the pointed toes of each shoe - this fashion actually originates from the Plantagenet era of English history but was associated with the nobility for some time. Banbury was situated at the top of a steep hill and in order to help carriages up the steep incline a white cock horse (a large stallion) was made available by the town's council to help with this task. When the Queen's carriage attempted to go up the hill a wheel broke and the Queen chose to mount the cock horse and ride to the Banbury cross. The people of the town had decorated the cock horse with ribbons and bells and provided minstrels to accompany her - "she shall have music wherever she goes". The massive stone cross at Banbury was unfortunately later destroyed by anti - Catholics who opposed the notion of pilgrimages.

Ring Around the Rosy

· · · · · · · · · · · · · · · ·

Ring-a-Ring o' Rosies
A Pocket full of Posies
"A-tishoo! A-tishoo!"
We all fall Down!

or

Ring Around the Rosy
A pocketful of posies
"Ashes, Ashes"
We all fall down!

· · · · · · · · · · · · · · · ·

Connections to the Bubonic Plague

The historical period of this rhyme dates back to the Great Plague of London in 1665 (bubonic plague). The symptoms of the plague included a rosy red rash in the shape of a ring on the skin (Ring around the rosy). Pockets and pouches were filled with sweet smelling herbs (posies) which were carried due to the belief that the disease was transmitted by bad smells. The term "Ashes Ashes" refers to the cremation of the dead bodies! The death rate was over 60% and the plague was only halted by the Great Fire of London in 1666 this killed the rats that carried the disease which was transmitted via water sources. The English version of "Ring around the Rosy" replaces ashes with (A-tishoo, A-tishoo) as violent sneezing was another symptom of the disease.

The Sceptics

The connection between this rhyme and the Bubonic Plague was made by several people including James Leasor in his 1961 non-fiction book called 'The Plague and the Fire'. Some people are sceptical of the plague related interpretations of this rhyme, many stating that words in the rhyme cannot be found in Middle English. The sceptics must be referring to the later version of the rhyme, Ring Around the Rosy, which possibly has American origins. The English version "Ring a ring o' rosies" uses the Middle English "o" as a shortening of the word "of". The word "posies" is first mentioned in a poem called 'Prothalamion or A Spousal Verse' by Edmund Spenser (1552-1599).

The Bubonic plague

In the Medieval era there were repeated outbreaks of the Bubonic plague and these were not just confined to highly populated towns such as London. The country area and villages were not exempt from the disease either - there was no hiding place. In the late sixteenth and seventeenth centuries victims of the Bubonic plague would be sealed in their houses. In later years houses containing victims were sometimes indicated with a red cross painted on the door with the words "God have Mercy". The houses would be locked and bolted from the outside. The victims were not allowed to leave and neither was anyone else allowed to enter. This action was tantamount to signing a death warrant for the whole family and one of the terrible consequences of the disease. Any victim of the Bubonic Plague would have to obtain a 'Certificate of Health' to resume normal life - if they recovered...

Sing a Song of Sixpence

Sing a song of sixpence a pocket full of rye,
Four and twenty blackbirds baked in a pie.
When the pie was opened the birds began to sing,
Oh wasn't that a dainty dish to set before the king?
The king was in his counting house counting out his money,
The queen was in the parlour eating bread and honey
The maid was in the garden hanging out the clothes,
When down came a blackbird and pecked off her nose!

First published in Tommy Thumb's Pretty Song Book c1744.

This children's action nursery rhyme creates an unusual image in a child's mind. Blackbirds and other song birds, were actually eaten as a delicacy especially during the Tudor period. However, a court jester may well have suggested to the court cook to bake a pie pastry crust and place this over some live blackbirds to surprise and amuse the King! It would not be unreasonable for the blackbirds to look for revenge hence "When down came a blackbird and pecked off her nose!" It is interesting to note that the references to the counting house and eating honey were the common man's perception of what a King and Queen spent their time doing. A pocketful of rye was purchased to feed birds. The nursery rhyme, when sung to a child, always ends with the tweaking of a child's nose!

There was a Crooked Man

. . . .

There was a crooked man and he walked a crooked mile,
He found a crooked sixpence upon a crooked stile.
He bought a crooked cat, which caught a crooked mouse.
And they all lived together in a little crooked house.

First appeared in print in c1842.

. . . .

This poem originates from the English Stuart history of King Charles I. The crooked man is reputed to be the Scottish General Sir Alexander Leslie. The General signed a Covenant securing religious and political freedom for Scotland. The 'crooked stile' referred to the border between England and Scotland. 'They all lived together in a little crooked house' refers to the fact that the English and Scots had at last come to an agreement. The words reflect the times when there was great animosity between the English and the Scots. The word crooked is pronounced as 'crookED' the emphasis being placed upon the 'ED' in the word. This was common in olde England and many references can be found using this type of pronunciation in the works of William Shakespeare (1564-1616).

There Was an Old Woman

There was an old woman who lived in a shoe,
She had so many children she didn't know what to do!
So she gave them some broth without any bread,
Then whipped them all soundly and sent them to bed!

First published in 1794.

At first glance the words to "There Was an Old Woman" would appear to be nonsense but in fact it is believed to have origins in English history. There are two choices of origin. The first relates to Queen Caroline (There was an old woman) wife of King George II who had eight children. The second version refers to King George who began the men's fashion for wearing white powdered wigs. He was consequently referred to as the old woman! The children were the members of parliament and the bed was the Houses of Parliament - even today the term 'whip' is used in the English Parliament to describe a member of Parliament who is tasked to ensure that all members 'toe the party line'. As a point of historical interest the wigs worn by women of the period were so large and unhygienic that it became necessary to include mousetraps in their construction!

King George II

Three Blind Mice

Three blind mice, three blind mice,
See how they run, see how they run,
They all ran after the farmer's wife,
Who cut off their tails with a carving knife,
Did you ever see such a sight in your life,
As three blind mice?

First published c1805.

The origin of the words to the Three Blind Mice are believed to be based in English history. The 'farmer's wife' refers to the daughter of King Henry VIII and Katherine of Aragon, Queen Mary I. Mary was a staunch Catholic and her violent persecution of Protestants led to the nickname of 'Bloody Mary'. The reference to 'farmer's wife' refers to the massive estates which she, and her husband King Philip of Spain, possessed. The 'three blind mice' were three noblemen who adhered to the Protestant faith who were convicted of plotting against the Queen - she did not have them dismembered and blinded as inferred in Three Blind Mice - but she did have them burnt at the stake!

Queen Mary I

PETER PETER PUMPKIN EATER

. . . .

People Rhymes

. . . .

Doctor Foster
Georgie Porgie
Hector Protector
Jack be Nimble (Jack b Nimble)
Jack and Jill
Jack Sprat (Jack Spratt)
Little Bo Peep
Little Boy Blue
Little Jack Horner
Little Miss Muffet
Little Tommy Tucker
Lucy Lockett
Mary had a Little Lamb
Mary Mary Quite Contrary
Old King Cole
Old Mother Hubbard
Peter Peter Pumpkin Eater
Simple Simon
The Grand Old Duke of York
The Queen of Hearts
Wee Willie Winkie

. . . .

Doctor Foster

. . . .

Doctor Foster , went to Gloucester
In a shower of rain.
He stepped in a puddle, right up to his middle
And never went there again!

. . . .

The Origins of the words from Doctor Foster
This poem clearly originates from England, with reference to the English county of Gloucestershire. It served as a warning to children in bygone days, prior to modern roads, that what may appear to be a shallow puddle could in fact be much deeper!

Who was Doctor Foster?
The origins reputedly lie in English history dating back to the Plantagenet monarchy of the 13th century when King Edward I (1239 - 1307) hereby known as Doctor Foster was thought to have visited Gloucester and fell from his horse into a large muddy puddle! He is said to have been so humiliated by this experience that he refused to ever visit Gloucester again!

King Edward I was a powerful man, over six foot tall - hence his nickname of Longshanks. He built many castle - fortresses in Wales as part of his strategy to conquer the Welsh who were lead by Llywelyn ap Gruffydd - Edward succeeded and Llywelyn became the last Prince of an independent Wales (c1223 - 1282).

Georgie Porgie

. . . .

Georgie Porgie pudding and pie,
Kissed the girls and made them cry
When the boys came out to play,
Georgie Porgie ran away.

. . . .

Naughty Georgie Porgie of the Stuart era

This English poem refers to the courtier George Villiers, 1st Duke of Buckingham (1592-1628). King James I took Villiers as his lover and nicknamed him "Steenie" (a reference to St. Stephen whom in the Bible is described as having the "face of an angel"). Villier's good looks also appealed to the ladies and his highly suspect morals were much in question!

Affair with the married lady - the Queen of France

Villiers most notorious affair was his liaison with Anne of Austria, (1601-1666) who was the Queen of France and married to the French King Louis XIII, badly injured both of their reputations. This however, was overlooked due to his great friendship with the English King, James I (1586 - 1625). He was disliked by both courtiers and commoners, not least for helping to arrange the marriage of King James' son to the French Catholic princess Henrietta Maria (1609-1669) - he later became King Charles I (1600-1649). George Villiers (Georgie Porgie) exercised great influence over the King who allowed him many liberties. Villiers private liaisons and political scheming were questioned and Parliament finally lost patience and stopped the King intervening on behalf of "Georgie Porgie". The romantic elements of George Villiers and Anne of Austria are featured in the novel 'The Three Musketeers' by Alexander Dumas.

George Villiers, Duke of Buckingham

Hector Protector

. . . .

Hector Protector was dressed all in green;
Hector Protector was sent to the Queen.
The Queen did not like him,
Nor more did the King;
So Hector Protector was sent back again.

. . . .

We originally believed that Hector Protector might relate to a Lord Protector of England, such as Oliver Cromwell or Edward Seymour, but the words of the rhyme simply did not relate to their stories. There was another, lesser known Protector of England, Richard, Duke of York (1411–1460). Richard, Duke of York was a claimant to the English throne. The reigning monarch was the weak and ineffective King Henry VI (1421–1471) who was married to the determined and highly ambitious Margaret of Anjou (1430–1482). Margaret ruled as Queen Consort and there was a bitter power struggle between her and Richard. In 1447 Richard was made heir presumptive to the throne but was sent to Ireland to get him out of the away. He returned to England in 1450 to fight against the growing ambitions of the Queen and her supporters. At this time Richard was able to secure control of the government as Protector due to the onset of the Kings insanity. The King recovered, and Richard was dismissed from his role as Protector and forced to flee to Ireland in 1459. He returned in 1460 but was killed at the Battle of Wakefield by the Queen's forces. By sheer coincidence, we also believe that Richard is possibly the character on whom the Grand old Duke of York nursery rhyme is based.

The weak King Henry VI

Jack be Nimble (Jack b Nimble)

Jack be nimble, Jack be quick
Jack jump over the candlestick.

First published in 1798.

Origin and History
The most commonly agreed origin for Jack be Nimble is the connection to Black Jack, an English pirate who was notorious for escaping from the authorities in the late 16th century hence 'Jack be nimble'. The words cannot be further analysed due to the brevity of the text but could be associated with the old tradition and sport of candle leaping which used to be practised at some English fairs.

Lace Makers and Candle Leaping?
The tradition of candle-leaping originated from an old game of jumping over fires. This dangerous game was banned and replaced by the far less dangerous sport of candle leaping. In Wendover there were lace-making schools (a good excuse for using children as slave labour). Here it was traditional to dance around the lace-makers great candlestick, and this led to jumping over the candlestick. Due to the cost of candles some employers only allowed the use of candles during the darkest months of the year and centred around Candlemas Day, known as the candle season. It is interesting to note that Jack be Nimble is now being referred to as Jack b Nimble - the influence of the modern day practise of texting!

Jack and Jill

· · · · · · · · · · · · · · · ·

Jack and Jill went up the hill to fetch a pail of water
Jack fell down and broke his crown
And Jill came tumbling after.
Up got Jack, and home did trot
As fast as he could caper
He went to bed and bound his head
With vinegar and brown paper.

First published in 1765.

· · · · · · · · · · · · · · · ·

Jack and Jill story - The French connection

The roots of this rhyme are set in France, Jack and Jill are said to be King Louis XVI - Jack -who was beheaded (lost his crown) followed by his Queen Marie Antoinette - Jill - (who came tumbling after). The words and lyrics were made more acceptable as a story for children by providing a happy ending! The actual beheadings occurred during the Reign of Terror in 1793, and the first publication date for the lyrics was 1795 - which ties-in with the history and origins. The Jack and Jill poem is also known as Jack and Gill - the misspelling of Gill is not uncommon in nursery rhymes as they are usually passed from generation to generation by word of mouth.

Death by Beheading!

On the gruesome subject of beheading it was the custom that following execution the executioner would hold up the severed head by the hair. This was not, as many people think, to show the crowd the head but in fact to show the head the crowd and it's own body! Consciousness remains for at least eight seconds after beheading until lack of oxygen causes unconsciousness and eventually death. The guillotine is associated with the French but the English were the first to use this device as described in the Mary Mary Quite Contrary Rhyme on page 68.

Vinegar and brown paper?

An application of vinegar and brown paper was used to treat various ills such as headaches, sprains and bruises. Chambers Encyclopaedia of 1868 recommended that "the heat and pain commonly experienced in sprains are often relieved by the local application of brown paper soaked in diluted vinegar."

The names Jack and Jill are often used as a general representation for a man and a woman.

William Shakespeare uses the names at the end of act three in 'A Midsummer Night's Dream' - "Jack shall have Jill; Nought shall go ill". Shakespeare also uses a similar reference in Love's Labour's Lost near the end of the play - "Our wooing doth not end like an old play; Jack hath not Jill".

A French Revolution execution Scene during the Reign of Terror

Jack Sprat (Jack Spratt)

Jack Sprat could eat no fat
His wife could eat no lean
And so betwixt the two of them
They licked the platter clean

Jack ate all the lean,
Joan ate all the fat.
The bone they picked it clean,
Then gave it to the cat

Jack Sprat was wheeling,
His wife by the ditch.
The barrow turned over,
And in she did pitch.

Says Jack, "She'll be drowned!"
But Joan did reply,
"I don't think I shall,
For the ditch is quite dry.".

First published in Mother Goose's Melody in 1765.

Origin to words of Jack Sprat can be found in British History

The Jack Sprat alluded to in this English poem is reputed to be King Charles I (1625-1649) and Henrietta Maria, his Queen (1609-1669). Apparently, when King Charles declared war on Spain, parliament refused to finance him "leaving him lean!" so his wife imposed an illegal war tax "to get some fat!" after the angered King (Jack Sprat) had dissolved Parliament.

The Robin Hood Legend!

Another interpretation of the Jack Sprat Nursery rhyme relates to the story of Richard I (Richard the Lionheart 1157 - 1199) and his younger brother King John (1166 - 1216). Both of whom feature strongly in the traditional legend of Robin Hood. In 1189 John (Jack Sprat), the younger brother of King Richard the Lionheart, married Joan the ambitious, greedy daughter - heiress of the Earl of Gloucester "Joan ate all the fat". When King Richard went on the third Crusade, from 1189 to 1192, his brother Prince John attempted to take the crown of England. Following this act John was known as a ruthless and treacherous usurper.

On his return from the crusade King Richard was shipwrecked which forced him into a dangerous route home through central Europe. Richard was captured and taken hostage near Vienna by Leopold V the Duke of Austria who accused Richard of arranging the murder of his cousin Conrad of Montserrat. Duke Leopold demanded a ransom of 150,000 marks for his safe return. John reluctantly had to raise the ransom, leaving the country destitute for years and reducing John's inheritance ("They picked it clean"). The ransom was paid and Richard was released.

John was crowned King of England following the death of Richard in 1199. He had his marriage to Joan annulled, she was never acknowledged as queen.

King Charles I whose constant disputes with
the Parliamentarians lead to the English
Civil War and his execution

Little Bo Peep

. . . .

Little Bo peep has lost her sheep
And doesn't know where to find them.
Leave them alone and they'll come home,
Bringing their tails behind them.
Little Bo peep fell fast asleep
And dreamt she heard them bleating,
But when she awoke, she found it a joke,
For they were all still fleeting.
Then up she took, her little crook
Determined for to find them.
She found them indeed, but it made her heart bleed,
For they left their tails behind them.
It happened one day, as Bo peep did stray
Into a meadow hard by,
There she espied their tails side by side
All hung on a tree to dry.
She heaved a sigh, and wiped her eye,
And over the hillocks went rambling,
And tried what she could,
As a shepherdess should,
To tack again each to its lambkin.

. . . .

The Little Bo Peep story

This rhyme builds the picture of a young shepherdess and the advice given to her by someone more experienced. It is interesting that the name of Little Bo Peep was derived from the derivative of the words bleat and sheep! There is a specific relevance to events in history for the origins of the Little Bo Peep rhyme. Until fields were enclosed with fences and hedges people used common land for grazing livestock. Children were often given the job of ensuring that animals did not wander off, hence nursery rhymes such as Little Bo Peep and Little Boy Blue. The morale of Little Bo Peep is that one must take responsibility of falling asleep or face the consequences.

Lambs tails were often removed to prevent 'fly strike' a fly that lays its eggs close to a sheeps bottom - the maggots then eat the flesh! The removal of the tails obviously took place whilst Bo Peep was asleep, or possibly over time they fell off with a ligature. Clearly, on seeing the sheep without tails she was dismayed and thought that she would get into trouble, therefore tried to re-unite the sheep with their tails by trying to find them.

The words of Little Bo Peep are quite interesting as they contain words that are an almost forgotten part of the English Language. Words such as espied, hillocks and lambkin can all be found in the story of Little Bo Peep.

Little Boy Blue

Cardinal Thomas Wolsey

Little Boy Blue come blow your horn,
The sheep's in the meadow the cow's in the corn.
But where's the boy who looks after the sheep?
He's under a haystack fast asleep.
Will you wake him? No, not I - for if I do, he's sure to cry.

A Connection with Tudor History?

The words and story cannot be positively connected to any historical figure in history but there is, however, a theory that Little Boy Blue refers to Cardinal Thomas Wolsey (1475-1530) dating back to English Tudor history and the reign of King Henry VIII. Wolsey was an extremely rich and arrogant self-made man with many enemies at court and was unpopular with the people of England. He was called the "Boy Bachelor" after obtaining his degree from Oxford at the unusually early age of fifteen. The expression "Blowing one's own horn" meaning to brag was certainly practised by Cardinal Wolsey. Between 1514 and 1525 he transformed a medieval manor into the magnificent Hampton Court Palace. It was an ostentatious display of his wealth and his power giving rise to the rhyme uttered by his enemies:

"Come ye to court? Which Court? The King's Court or Hampton Court?"

The anti-Wolsey propaganda worked and in 1529 Henry declared all of Wolsey's lands and possessions forfeit and they became the property of the Crown. At this time England was a prosperous nation largely through the wool trade. The export taxes on wool had augmented both Henry's treasury and Wolsey's assets. The words "where's the boy who looks after the sheep?" could refer to Wolsey's concern with lining his own coffers as opposed to that of the country. The cardinal's robes were scarlet but Wolsey's Blazon of Arms included the blue faces of four leopards - perhaps this was why the title of the rhyme is Little Boy Blue? The Little Boy Blue rhyme may have been a secret message of dissent concerning the greed of the statesman prior to his downfall. Open criticism of the Cardinal would have lead to imprisonment, confiscation of property or even death. Another rhyme reputedly relating to Cardinal Wolsey is Old Mother Hubbard.

A simpler explanation for the emergence of this rhyme is that until fields were enclosed with fences and hedges people used common land for grazing livestock. Children were often given the job of ensuring that animals did not wander off hence Nursery Rhymes such as Little Bo Peep and Little Boy Blue.

Little Jack Horner

Little Jack Horner sat in the corner
Eating his Christmas pie,
He put in his thumb and pulled out a plum
And said "What a good boy am I!"

First published in 1725.

. . . .

16th Century History origin of the Little Jack Horner story

Little Jack Horner was reputed to have been the Steward to Richard Whiting (1461 - 1539) the Bishop of Glastonbury. The Steward had an important role and was responsible for managing the household, collecting taxes and keeping accounts.

The Church, the King and the Gold

Glastonbury was the largest and wealthiest Abbey in England and this Benedictine Monastery owned extensive lands and manors in the county of Somerset. Between 1536 and 1540, after breaking away from the Catholic Church, King Henry VIII and his chief minister Thomas Cromwell set about the systematic Dissolution of all of the Monasteries in England. The reason for this was to loot the monasteries of their gold and silver and seize the monastic lands. By 1539 Glastonbury was the only religious house left in Somerset and it was only a matter of time before Glastonbury Abbey was also seized.

The Bribe

It is rumoured that the Bishop tried to bribe the King. He sent his Steward, Jack Horner, with a gift of twelve title deeds to various English manorial estates. The deeds were said to have been secreted in a pie (valuables were often hidden in this bizarre fashion to thwart thieves). Little Jack Horner realised that the bribe would do no good and was said to have stolen the deeds to the manor of Mells (it being the real 'plum' of the twelve manors).

The Traitor and the Execution

The remaining eleven manors were given to the crown but to no avail. The old Bishop was convicted of treason for remaining loyal to Rome. The jury included his treacherous steward Horner who found Bishop Whiting guilty and sent the old man to a terrible death of being hung, drawn and quartered on Glastonbury Tor. The Abbey was destroyed. Following the destruction of the abbey the steward, Horner, moved into the Manor of Mells. Whether Horner actually stole the deeds to the Manor or was rewarded with them for helping to convict the Bishop of Glastonbury is not known but the Manor of Mells became the property of the Horner family who lived there until the 20th century.

. . . .

Little Miss Muffet

. . . .

John Knox - The spider?

Little Miss Muffet sat on a tuffet
Eating her curds and whey,
Along came a spider,
Who sat down beside her
And frightened Miss Muffet away!

Published in 1805 in a book called 'Songs for the Nursery'.

. . . .

Who was Little Miss Muffet?
One theory is that Little Miss Muffet was a small girl whose name was Patience Muffet. Her stepfather, Dr. Muffet (1553-1604) was a famous entomologist who wrote the first scientific catalogue of British insects. Whilst eating her breakfast of curds and whey Little Miss Muffet was frightened by one of his spiders and ran away! This particular Nursery Rhyme of Little Miss Muffet reputedly dates back to the late 16th century as indicated by the birth date of Dr Muffet.

Another theory is that the staunch Roman Catholic Mary, Queen of Scots (1543-1587) was the Little Miss Muffet referred to in the rhyme and that the Scottish religious reformer John Knox (1510-1572) was the spider who frightened her away. Mary Queen of Scots eventually fled from Scotland due to the hatred of the religious reformers and is reputed to have said: "I'll fear the prayers of John Knox more than all the assembled armies of Europe".

What are Curds and whey?
They are the lumps and liquid similar to those found in cottage cheese. It is made by adding vinegar to warm milk. The curds separate from the whey as the ingredients are stirred. Curds are the milk solids and the whey is the liquid that is poured off.

Little Tommy Tucker

Little Tommy Tucker sings for his supper,
What shall we give him? Brown bread and butter.
How shall he cut it without a knife?
How shall he marry without a wife?

The earliest publication of this rhyme is from
Tommy Thumb's Pretty Song Book (c. 1744).

Who, or what, was Little Tommy Tucker?
Little 'Tommy Tucker' referred to in the words of this nursery rhyme was a
colloquial term that was commonly used to describe orphans. The orphans were
often reduced to begging or 'singing for their supper'. The reference to Little
Tommy Tucker marrying and the lack of a wife reflects the difficulty of any
orphan being able to marry due to their exceptionally low standing within the
community. As a point of interest the name 'Tucker' dates back to the Anglo-
Saxon tribes of England and was used to describe a person who cleaned &
thickened cloth. The word derived from the Old English word tucian, which
originally meant to torment - the tucker's job involved beating and trampling
cloth in water.

Lucy Lockett

· · · · · · · · · · · · · · · · ·

Lucy Locket lost her pocket,
Kitty Fisher found it;
Not a penny was there in it,
Only ribbon round it.

· · · · · · · · · · · · · · · · ·

The words of this nursery rhyme are reputed to have been based on people and places in London during the 1700's. Lucy Lockett was believed to be a barmaid at the Cock Public House in Fleet Street, London. This pub, or alehouse was first established in 1554 and rebuilt in 1888. Samuel Pepys mentioned the Cock Alehouse in his diary which stated:

April 23 1668 – "To the Cock Alehouse and drank and ate a lobster, and sang..."

Kitty Fisher was a famous courtesan during the reign of King Charles II. Catherine Maria 'Kitty' Fisher died in 1767. Her lifestyle was described as follows:

"She lives in the greatest possible splendor, spends twelve thousand pounds a year, and she is the first of her social class to employ liveried servants..."

The Pocket referred to was the old Middle English word for a pouch or a small bag. The implication is that poor Lucy Lockett made very little money as opposed to the similarly employed Kitty who was envied for her great beauty and vast wealth.

Mary had a Little Lamb

· · · · · · · · · · · · · · · · ·

Thomas Edison

Mary had a little lamb its fleece was white as snow;
And everywhere that Mary went, the lamb was sure to go.
It followed her to school one day, which was against the rule;
It made the children laugh and play, to see a lamb at school.
And so the teacher turned it out, but still it lingered near,
And waited patiently about till Mary did appear.
"Why does the lamb love Mary so?" the eager children cry;
"Why, Mary loves the lamb, you know" the teacher did reply.

· · · · · · · · · · · · · · · · ·

Mary had a little lamb - use of language
The words of the American nursery rhyme Mary had a Little Lamb would appeal
to small children and introduces imagery of similes (white as snow) as part of
use of the English language. The words also convey the hopeful adage that love
is reciprocated. No specific historical connection can be traced to the words of
Mary had a Little Lamb but it can be confirmed that the rhyme is American
as the words were written by Sarah Hale, of Boston, in 1830. An interesting
historical note - the words of this rhyme were the first ever recorded by Thomas
Edison, on tin foil, via his phonograph.

Mary Mary Quite Contrary

· · · · · · · · · · · · · · · · ·

Mary Mary quite contrary,
How does your garden grow?
With silver bells and cockle shells
And pretty maids all in a row.

· · · · · · · · · · · · · · · · ·

The origins are steeped in history... Bloody Mary

The Mary mentioned in this traditional English nursery rhyme is reputed to be Mary Tudor, or Bloody Mary, who was the daughter of King Henry VIII and his first wife Katherine of Aragon. Queen Mary was a staunch Catholic and the garden referred to is an allusion to graveyards which were increasing in size with those who dared to continue to adhere to the Protestant faith - Protestant martyrs.

Instruments of Torture!

The silver bells and cockle shells referred to in the Nursery Rhyme were colloquialisms for instruments of torture. The 'silver bells' were thumbscrews which crushed the thumb between two hard surfaces by the tightening of a screw. The 'cockleshells' were believed to be instruments of torture which were attached to the genitals!

The " Maids" or Maiden was the original guillotine!

The 'maids' were a device to behead people called the Maiden. Beheading a victim was fraught with problems. It could take up to 11 blows to actually sever the head, the victim often resisted and had to be chased around the scaffold. Margaret Pole (1473 - 1541), Countess of Salisbury did not go willingly to her death and had to be chased and hacked at by the Executioner. These problems led to the invention of a mechanical instrument (now known as the guillotine) called the Maiden - shortened to Maids in the Mary Mary Nursery Rhyme. The Maiden had long been in use in England before Lord Morton Regent of Scotland, during the minority of James VI, had a copy constructed from the Maiden which had been used in Halifax in Yorkshire. Ironically, Lord Morton fell from favour and was the first to experience the Maiden in Scotland!

Executions!

Another form of execution during Mary's reign was being burnt at the stake - a terrible punishment much used during the Spanish Inquisition. The English hated the Spanish and dreaded the idea of an English Inquisition. The executions during the reign of Bloody Mary were therefore viewed with a greater fear of the Spanish than the executions themselves - it is interesting to note that executions during Mary's reign totalled less than 300 an insignificant amount compared to those ordered by her father King Henry VIII which are believed to have numbered tens of thousands!

Old King Cole

Old King Cole was a merry old soul,
and a merry old soul was he;
He called for his pipe in the middle of the night
And he called for his fiddlers three.
Every fiddler had a fine fiddle,
and a very fine fiddle had he;
Oh there's none so rare as can compare
With King Cole and his fiddlers three.

Who was Old King Cole?

The origins of this rhyme date back to the 3rd century. There is considerable confusion regarding the origins of Old King Cole as there are three possible contenders who were Celtic Kings of Britain, all who share the name Coel (which is the Celtic word for the English name Cole). "Historia Regum Britanniae" (History of the Kings of Britain) by Geoffrey of Monmouth (1110-1155) refers to a King Cole as a king of the Britons.

Our research details the contenders as follows:

Coel Godhebog (Cole the Magnificent - b.220 Decurion of Rome) was the Lord of Colchester (the word Colchester means 'Cole's Castle'). The Romans had conquered Britain during this period and Coel Godhebog was a Decurion meaning member of the municipal Senate in Ancient Rome who ran a local government. Gaius Flavius Valerius Constantius (250-306) was an Emperor of the Western Roman Empire (305-306). According to the Historia Regum Britanniae, Constantius was sent to Britain in 296AD, where his liaison with Helena, apparently the daughter of Coel Godhebog, produced a son who became Constantine the Great.

Coel Hen (Coel the Old c.350 - c.420), called Coel the Old due to his longevity, was also the Lord of Colchester and a Decurion. This was the time of the Decline of the Roman Empire and the Roman officials abandoned Britain and returned to Italy which was under attack by the Goths. Coel Hen was therefore believed to be the last Decurion. This man is probably the main contender as 'Old King Cole' due to the name he was given - Coel the Old.

St. Ceneu ap Coel (Born c382), the son of Coel Hen. Ceneu appears to have been made a Saint because he upheld the old Christian ways against pagan invaders. He used Saxon mercenaries to help with this quest. He was named in the Historia Regum Britanniae as attending the coronation of King Arthur who became the 'One King' of the Britons.

The Origins

The History of the Ancient Britons is reflected in the origins of Old King Cole encompassing the ancient times and dynasties of the Celts, the Romans, the Saxons and King Arthur. The Tudor dynasty, starting with King Henry VII, claimed to descend from Old King Cole's royal lineage in attempt to further legitimise the Royal House of Tudor's claim to the English throne. One of the main sources of information regarding the Ancient Britons is taken from the works by Geoffrey of Monmouth. Geoffrey lived many years later in the 1100's and much of his history on the pre-Saxon kings of Britain is based on Celtic legends - thus adding to the confusion regarding the origins of Old King Cole. This rhyme was first published in William King's 'Useful Transactions in Philosophy' in 1708.

Old Mother Hubbard

. . . .

Old Mother Hubbard
Went to the cupboard
To get her poor doggie a bone,
When she got there
The cupboard was bare
So the poor little doggie had none.

First published in 1805.

. . . .

Origins of Old Mother Hubbard lyrics in British history

The Old Mother Hubbard referred to in this rhyme's words are reputed to allude to the famous Cardinal Wolsey. Cardinal Thomas Wolsey was the most important statesman and churchman of the Tudor history period in 16th century England. Cardinal Wolsey proved to be a faithful servant but displeased the King, Henry VIII, by failing to facilitate the King's divorce from Queen Katherine of Aragon, who had been his queen of many years. The reason for seeking the divorce was to enable King Henry VIII to marry Anne Boleyn, with whom he was passionately in love. In the Old Mother Hubbard song King Henry was the "doggie" and the "bone" refers to the divorce (and not money as many believe). The cupboard relates to the Catholic Church although the subsequent divorce arranged by Thomas Cramner resulted in the break with Rome, the consequent formation of the English Protestant church and the demise of Old Mother Hubbard, the unfortunate Cardinal Wolsey. Another rhyme which reputedly relates to Cardinal Wolsey is Little Boy Blue.

Katherine of Aragon

Cardinal Wolsey

Peter Peter Pumpkin Eater

Peter Peter pumpkin eater,
Had a wife and couldn't keep her!
He put her in a pumpkin shell,
And there he kept her very well!

First published in Boston, Massachusetts in 1825.

The lyrics of this rhyme (unlike most) originate not in Europe, but in America. This rhyme has become known to British children only in recent years as for most British children it has only just become clear exactly what a pumpkin is! As it is not indigenous to the British shores the vast majority of the British population have never eaten pumpkin! The American tradition of dressing up for Halloween (and the subsequent use of the pumpkin for making lanterns) together with 'Trick or Treat' has only reached our shores a few years ago.

Whilst the Nursery Rhyme 'Peter Peter Pumpkin Eater' originated in America it is possible that it was adapted from an old English rhyme called Eeper Weeper Chimbly Sweeper:

Eeper Weeper, chimbly sweeper, Had a wife but couldn't keep her.
Had another, didn't love her, Up the chimbly he did shove her.

Simple Simon

Simple Simon met a pieman going to the fair;
Said Simple Simon to the pieman "Let me taste your ware"
Said the pieman to Simple Simon "Show me first your penny"
Said Simple Simon to the pieman "Sir, I have not any!"

First published in c1744.

Origin of the lyrics to Simple Simon

In this modern era we tend to believe that fast and convenience food is a recent invention. However, this type of food dates back to the Romans when fast food was sold in the Roman Colosseum. In England fast food, such as pies, were sold from trays by street sellers. A fair was an extremely popular place to sell 'your ware'. The tradition and history of fairs dates back to Medieval England. The modern day version of Simple Simon can be found in the song and a game where children have to do exactly what Simple Simon says.

Southwark Fair, London.

The Grand Old Duke of York

. . . .

The Grand old Duke of York he had ten thousand men
He marched them up to the top of the hill
And he marched them down again.
When they were up, they were up
And when they were down, they were down
And when they were only halfway up
They were neither up nor down.

. . . .

The Wars of the Roses

The origin to the words of this rhyme are believed to date back to the Plantagenet dynasty in the 15th century and refer mockingly to the defeat of Richard, "The Grand Old Duke of York" at the Battle of Wakefield (December 1, 1460) during the Wars of the Roses (1453 – 1487). The Wars of the Roses were between two royal factions: the house of York (whose symbol was a white rose) and the house of Lancaster (whose symbol was a red rose). Richard, Duke of York, was the Protector of England and claimant to the English throne. The Duke of York and his army marched to his castle at Sandal where Richard took up a defensive position against the Lancastrian army. Sandal Castle was built on top of the site of an old Norman motte and Bailey fortress. Its massive earthworks stood 33 feet (10m) above the original ground level ("he marched them up to the top of the hill"). In a moment of madness he left his stronghold in the castle and went down to make a direct attack on the Lancastrians "he marched them down again". His army was overwhelmed and Richard, the Duke of York, was killed.

Motte & Bailey castle fortress

The Queen of Hearts

· · · · · · · · · · · · · · · · ·

The Queen of Hearts she made some tarts
all on a summer's day;
The Knave of Hearts he stole the tarts
and took them clean away.
The King of Hearts called for the tarts
and beat the Knave full sore
The Knave of Hearts brought back the tarts
and vowed he'd steal no more.

First appeared in print in 1782.

· · · · · · · · · · · · · · · · ·

Alice in Wonderland
The term and famous reference to the 'Queen of Hearts' can be found in the work of Lewis G. Carroll in his book entitled 'Alice in Wonderland' which was first published in 1805. The Queen of Hearts in this story was famous for the saying "Off with their heads!" when she was annoyed with her servants.

The Queen of Hearts Playing Card
Decks of cards depicting illustrations of Kings and Queens can be traced back to France in 1650. These French cards portrayed the Queen of Hearts as Judith from the Bible. This depiction of Judith was to convey the attribute of courage. In the Bible Judith killed the Assyrian General Holofernes.

Princess Diana
In more recent history the term the Queen of Hearts was used by Princess Diana during her famous interview with Martin Bashir. Princess Diana stated her preference to the title the Queen of Hearts to that of Queen of England. Princess Diana is now lovingly referred to as the Queen of Hearts.

Author, Lewis Carroll.

Wee Willie Winkie

· · · · · · · · · · · · · · · · ·

Wee Willie Winkie runs through the town,
Upstairs and downstairs in his nightgown,
Tapping at the window and crying through the lock,
Are all the children in their beds, it's past eight o'clock?

Author William Miller (1810 - 1872) First publication date 1841.

· · · · · · · · · · · · · · · · ·

The intention of the words to Wee Willie Winkie was to teach children to associate every day tasks with their own lives. Before the days of the radio, television and the internet great reliance was put upon the Town Crier to pass on the latest news and information. 'Wee Willie Winkie' was the children's version of the Town Crier.

There was once a Curfew Law in England that dates back to the reign of King Alfred the Great which was subsequently adopted by William the Conqueror. The Curfew Law forbade anyone to leave their homes after 8 o'clock and was signified by the ringing of a Curfew Bell. This law and infringement of liberties lasted until 1103. However, the ringing of the Curfew Bell became an English tradition so much so that 'Curfew' bells are still rung in many English towns to this very day.

THE LION AND THE UNICORN

Useful, Historic & Weather Lore Rhymes

. . . .

Monday's Child
Remember Remember the Fifth of November
The Lion and the Unicorn
When Adam delved and Eve span
Red Sky at Night
St. Swithin's day

Epic Tales

. . . .

London bridge is falling down
London bridge is broken down
Oranges and Lemons
London Bells

Monday's Child

. . . .

Monday's child is fair of face,
Tuesday's child is full of grace,
Wednesday's child is full of woe,
Thursday's child has far to go,
Friday's child is loving and giving,
Saturday's child works hard for his living,
And the child that is born on the Sabbath day
Is bonny and blithe, and good and gay.

First published in A. E. Bray's Traditions of Devonshire in 1838.

. . . .

The words of Monday's child poem are used to associate children with the pattern and different names to the days of week. The poem is very popular but the actual words are not so well known. We have all learnt the days of the week as the rhyme intended but we cannot seem to remember the qualities associated with being born on individual days. Sunday was traditionally referred to as the 'Sabbath day' so there is no specific reference to Sunday. Sunday is considered the last day of the week (weekend) in many countries such as the United Kingdom although other countries, including the United States and Japan, it is considered the first day of the week. Another rhyme used to help us remember the number of days in every month is as follows:

Thirty days hath September,
April, June, and November;
February has twenty-eight alone.
All the rest have thirty-one,
Excepting leap year, that's the time
When February has twenty-nine

Remember Remember the Fifth of November

. . . .

Remember remember the fifth of November
Gunpowder, treason and plot.
I see no reason why gunpowder, treason
Should ever be forgot'n. . .

. . . .

Guy Fawkes & The Gunpowder Plot

The words refer to Guy Fawkes with origins in 17th century English history. On the 5th November 1605 Guy Fawkes was caught in the cellars of the Houses of Parliament with several dozen barrels of gunpowder. Guy Fawkes was subsequently tried as a traitor, with his co-conspirators, for plotting against the government. He was tried by Judge Popham who came to London specifically for the trial from his country manor Littlecote House in Hungerford, Gloucestershire. Fawkes was sentenced to death and the form of the execution was one of the most horrendous ever practised (hung, drawn and quartered) which reflected the serious nature of the crime of treason.

The Tradition begins...

The following year in 1606 it became an annual custom for the King and Parliament to commission a sermon to commemorate the event. Lancelot Andrewes delivered the first of many Gunpowder Plot Sermons. This practice, together with the nursery rhyme, ensured that this crime would never be forgotten. Hence the words " Remember, remember the fifth of November" the poem is sometimes referred to as 'Please to remember the fifth of November'. It serves as a warning to each new generation that treason will never be forgotten. In England the 5th of November is still commemorated each year with fireworks and bonfires culminating with the burning of effigies of Guy Fawkes (the guy).

The 'guys' are made by children by filling old clothes with crumpled newspapers to look like a man. Tradition allows British children to display their 'guys' to passers-by and ask for " A penny for the guy".

The Gunpowder Plot conspirators. From the left; Thomas Bates, Robert Wintour, Christopher Wright, John Wright, Thomas Percy, Guy Fawkes, Robert Catesby and Thomas Wintour.

The Lion and the Unicorn

· · · · · · · · · · · · · · · ·

The lion and the unicorn were fighting for the crown
The lion beat the unicorn all around the town.
Some gave them white bread, and some gave them brown;
Some gave them plum cake and drummed them out of town.

· · · · · · · · · · · · · · · ·

The Lion and the Unicorn dates from 1603 when King James VI of Scotland became James I of England unifying the Scottish and English kingdoms. The lion stands for England and the unicorn for Scotland. The 'Virgin Queen' Elizabeth I named the son of Mary Queen of Scots, James, as her heir. The union of the two countries required a new royal coat of arms combining those of England, which featured two lions, and Scotland whose coat of arms featured two Unicorns. A compromise was made, thus the British coat of arms now has one Lion and one Unicorn and the rhyme about "The Lion and the Unicorn" was created.

The picture depicts the Lion (with the crown) and the Unicorn Coat of Arms.

The centre of the Arms depicts the lions of England in the first and fourth quarters, the lion of Scotland in the second and the Harp of Ireland in the third quarter. The motto around the centre means:
"Evil to him who evil thinks" which relates to the Order of the Garter. The motto at the bottom means: "God and my Right".

When Adam delved and Eve span

. . . .

"When Adam delved, and Eve span
Who was then a gentleman?"

. . . .

This is one of the oldest known rhymes and can be dated to the English Peasant Revolt of 1381. At this time the English had suffered horrifically due to the deadly Black Death (Bubonic Plague) during which as many as a third of the population had died. The peasants realised that they were now important in society. This seemingly innocent Rhyme was uttered and muttered by the peasants of the land. Like many political rhymes this was easy to remember and makes use of the simple riddle. The seeds of an English Revolution had been sown. The peasants felt oppressed and called for the abolition of feudal obligations - serfdom. They wanted freedom from servitude, controlled wages, and unfair taxes.

The Rulers
During this period England was ruled by the young Plantagenet King Richard II who gained the throne 4 years before in 1377. The peasants were loyal to the King and their hatred was centred on his uncle, the rich and powerful John of Gaunt.

The Rebels
The Kentish leaders of the Revolt were Robert Cave, Abel Ker, Jack Straw, Thomas Farringdon and Wat Tyler and the rebellion soon spread to Essex and London. A priest called John Ball stirred the flame of revolution even higher by preaching to the peasants and encouraging them to call for justice.

The Story
The peasants marched on London whilst the boy-King Richard II and his Court including the Earl of Derby (the future Henry IV), John of Gaunt's son, Sir Thomas Percy (admiral), and Sir Thomas Walworth (Lord Mayor of London) had fled to the Tower of London for safety. King Richard met the rebels at Blackheath and agreed to their demands - many of the peasants peacefully returned to their homes. The remaining peasants led by Wat Tyler met with the King again at Smithfield. Wat Tyler was wounded and captured - he was later beheaded by Mayor Walworth and his men. John Ball met an even more horrific fate and was hung, drawn and quartered. The King had won the day and the rebellion was crushed. But the rhyme which sparked the English Revolution is still remembered today.

Red Sky at Night

· · · · · · · · · · · · · · · · ·

Red sky at night,
Shepherd's delight;
Red sky at morning,
Shepherd's warning.

or

Red sky at night,
Sailor's delight;
Red sky at morning,
Sailor's warning.

· · · · · · · · · · · · · · · · ·

The practical origins for this English nursery rhyme are based on weather predictions and how a red sky at night would indicate fair weather on the following day. In England the words refer to a shepherd who would say that a red sky in the morning was suggesting inclement weather to follow. In America the words relate to a sailor. It should be remembered that there were no weather forecasts, as such, in days gone by and those with the most knowledge and experience, such as Sailors and Shepherds, whose lives were dependant on the weather were fully conversant with changing weather patterns such as a "Red Sky at Night".

The original origins of this Nursery Rhyme can be traced to the Bible: Matthew 16:2-3 2 - He answered and said unto them, "When it is evening, ye say, It will be fair weather: for the sky is red." 3 - "And in the morning, It will be foul weather to day: for the sky is red and lowering. O ye hypocrites, ye can discern the face of the sky; but can ye not discern the signs of the times?"

St. Swithin's Day

. . . .

St. Swithin's day if thou dost rain
For forty days it will remain
St. Swithin's day if thou be fair
For forty days 'twill rain nae mair.

. . . .

The words and lyrics of this nursery rhyme reflect the old wive's tale that if it rains on St. Swithin's day then it will continue to rain for a further forty days. St. Swithin's Day falls on 15th July. St. Swithin, or Swithun was born circa 800 and died AD862. He was a Saxon Bishop of Winchester and was originally buried, at his request, in a humble outside grave. Nine years later on 15 July 971, the monks moved his remains to a magnificent shrine inside the Cathedral. Legend says that during the ceremony it began to rain and continued to do so for forty days. The Shrine of St. Swithun, together with the tomb of Alfred the Great, made Winchester Cathedral a principal place of pilgrimage in England. The shrine was destroyed in 1538 by King Henry VIII' s men during the Dissolution of the Monasteries.

King Henry VIII whose men were responsible for the
destruction of the Shrine of St. Swithin

London Bridge is Falling Down

· · · · · · · · · · · · · · · ·

London Bridge is falling down, Falling down, falling down,
London Bridge is falling down, My fair Lady.

Build it up with wood and clay, Wood and clay, wood and clay,
Build it up with wood and clay, My fair Lady.

Wood and clay will wash away, Wash away, wash away,
Wood and clay will wash away, My fair Lady.

Build it up with bricks and mortar, Bricks and mortar, bricks and mortar,
Build it up with bricks and mortar, My fair Lady.

Bricks and mortar will not stay, Will not stay, will not stay,
Bricks and mortar will not stay, My fair Lady.

Build it up with iron and steel, Iron and steel, iron and steel,
Build it up with iron and steel, My fair Lady.

Iron and steel will bend and bow, Bend and bow, bend and bow,
Iron and steel will bend and bow, My fair Lady.

Build it up with silver and gold, Silver and gold, silver and gold,
Build it up with silver and gold, My fair Lady.

Silver and gold will be stolen away, Stolen away, stolen away,
Silver and gold will be stolen away, My fair Lady.

Set a man to watch all night, Watch all night, watch all night,
Set a man to watch all night, My fair Lady.

Suppose the man should fall asleep, Fall asleep, fall asleep,
Suppose the man should fall asleep? My fair Lady.

Give him a pipe to smoke all night, Smoke all night, smoke all night,
Give him a pipe to smoke all night, My fair Lady.

· · · · · · · · · · · · · · · ·

The Wooden Bridge

The London Bridge is falling down nursery rhyme is based on the one of the most famous landmarks in London. Its history can be traced to the Roman occupation of England in the first century. The first London Bridge was made of wood and clay and was fortified or re-built with the various materials mentioned in the children's nursery rhyme. Many disasters struck the bridges - Viking invaders destroyed the bridge in the 1000's which led to a fortified design, complete with a drawbridge. Building materials changed due to the many fires that broke out on the bridge.

The Stone Bridge

The first stone bridge was designed by Peter de Colechurch and built in 1176. It took 33 years to build and featured twenty arches the dimensions of which were sixty feet high and thirty feet wide and was complete with tower and gates. The flow of the Thames under the bridge was used to turn water wheels below the arches for grinding grain. By the 1300's the bridge contained 140 shops, some of which were more than three stories high. (The reference to Silver and Gold in the rhyme relates to the trading which was conducted on the bridge). London Bridge survived the Great Fire of London in 1666 but its arches and foundations were weakened. (Buildings with thatched roofs were banned in London following the Great Fire of 1666 and this ban was only lifted with the construction of the New Globe Theatre in 1994.

The Modern Re-builds

In the 1820s a new London Bridge was built on another site, north of the old one. This new bridge opened in 1831 and the old bridge was demolished. In the 1960s yet another London Bridge was built. The London Bridge of 1831 was transported, stone by stone, to Lake Havasu in Arizona, USA.

London Bridge, complete with houses, gatehouse and church

London Bridge is Broken Down

· · · · · · · · · · · · · · · ·

London bridge is broken down, Dance over my Lady Lee,
London bridge is broken down, With a gay ladye.

How shall we build it up again? Dance over my Lady Lee,
How shall we build it up again? With a gay ladye.

We'll build it up with gravel and stone, Dance over my Lady Lee,
We'll build it up with gravel and stone, With a gay ladye.

Gravel and stone will be washed away, Dance over my Lady Lee,
Gravel and stone will be washed away, With a gay ladye.

We'll build it up with iron and steel, Dance over my Lady Lee,
We'll build it up with iron and steel, With a gay ladye.

Iron and steel will bend and break, Dance over my Lady Lee,
Iron and steel will bend and break, With a gay ladye.

We'll build it up with silver and gold, Dance over my Lady Lee,
We'll build it up with silver and gold, With a gay ladye.

Silver and gold will be stolen away, Dance over my Lady Lee,
Silver and gold will be stolen away, With a gay ladye.

We'll set a man to watch it then, Dance over my Lady Lee,
We'll set a man to watch it then, With a gay ladye.

Suppose the man should fall asleep, Dance over my Lady Lee,
Suppose the man should fall asleep, With a gay ladye.

We'll put a pipe into his mouth, Dance over my Lady Lee,
We'll put a pipe into his mouth, With a gay ladye.

· · · · · · · · · · · · · · · ·

Who was Lady Lee?

The origins of this nursery rhyme are truly fascinating and have roots in the extraordinary events surrounding King Henry VIII of England (1491-1547) and his second, tragic, wife Anne Boleyn. 'The Lady Lee' referred to in the Nursery Rhyme was, in fact, Lady Margaret Wyatt, the sister of Thomas Wyatt the poet. She married Sir Anthony Lee of Quarrendon and thus became Lady Lee. The Wyatts were neighbours of the Boleyn family and Anne and Margaret were childhood friends.

Anne Boleyn

As Anne rose in power Margaret accompanied her and become a trusted lady-in-waiting. When Anne was accused of bigamy Thomas Wyatt was accused with her, but he was later released. Margaret, Lady Lee, stayed with Anne Boleyn until her execution and attended the ill-fated queen on the scaffold. This nursery rhyme can be described as an allegory - a description of one thing under the image of another. The words are believed to describe the rise and fall of Anne Boleyn (the gay ladye) and the lyrics use the name of Lady Lee to clearly identify the central character, Anne Boleyn.

The Hidden Secrets in Nursery Rhymes

Many nursery rhymes have secret, hidden, meanings and allude to people and events in history. Anne Boleyn was hated by the common people of England, due to her haughty manner and the common folk's strong allegiance to Henry VIII's first wife, Katherine of Aragon. Open criticism of Anne was approved and encouraged during the reigns of Henry VIII and his eldest daughter Mary (Bloody Mary - Henry and Katherine's daughter). But when Queen Elizabeth I ascended to the throne all such approval and criticism stopped - the new Queen was the daughter of Henry VIII and Anne Boleyn. The words and lyrics of London Bridge is Broken Down are thus explained.

King Henry VIII & Anne Boleyn

Oranges and Lemons

. . . .

"Oranges and lemons" say the Bells of St. Clement's
"You owe me five farthings" say the Bells of St. Martin's
"When will you pay me?" say the Bells of Old Bailey
"When I grow rich" say the Bells of Shoreditch
"When will that be?" say the Bells of Stepney
"I do not know" say the Great Bells of Bow
"Here comes a Candle to light you to Bed
Here comes a Chopper to Chop off your Head
Chip chop chip chop - the Last Man's Dead."

. . . .

History and Origin

The exact date of origin is unknown but there was a Square Dance called Oranges and Lemons dating back to 1665. Unfortunately, there is no known record of the lyrics which accompanied the dance but it is likely that the words are similar to the nursery rhyme. Oranges and Lemons is a shortened version of another poem, called London Bells and the words relate to some of the many churches in London. The tune that accompanies the lyrics emulates the sound of the ringing of the individual church bells.

The words have been much loved by numerous generations of children as they play the game of Oranges and Lemons. The end of the game culminates in a child being caught between the joined arms of two others, emulating the act of chopping off their head! The reason for the sinister last three lines are easily explained - they are a reference to executions...

Execution Procession at Tyburn, London

The Tyburn Gallows
In 1783 the infamous public execution gallows (the Tyburn-Tree) was moved from Tyburn-Gate (Marble Arch) to Newgate. Newgate was the name of a notorious prison for both criminals and debtors hence the line "When will you pay me?" The move was necessary to reduce problems caused by the crowds, often exceeding 100,000, who gathered along the execution procession route, stretching the three miles from Newgate Prison to the gallows.

Newgate Prison
The 'Bells of Old Bailey', or more accurately the tenor bell of St Sepulchre, had been utilised prior to 1783 to time the executions. However, after the gallows were moved, Newgate prison (now the site of the Old Bailey) obtained its own bell. The unfortunate prisoners would await execution on 'Death Row', and were informed of their fate by the Bellman of St. Sepulchre. At midnight, on the Sunday night prior to their execution, the Bellman made his rounds by candle light "Here comes the candle to light you to bed". As he passed the cells he rang the 'Execution Bell' (a large hand bell) and the recited the following poem:

> *All you that in the condemned hole do lie,*
> *Prepare you for tomorrow you shall die;*
> *Watch all and pray: the hour is drawing near*
> *That you before the Almighty must appear;*
> *Examine well yourselves in time repent,*
> *That you may not to eternal flames be sent.*
> *And when St. Sepulchre's Bell in the morning tolls*
> *The Lord above have mercy on your soul.*

The executions commenced at nine o'clock Monday morning following the first toll of the tenor bell.

'On the Wagon'
The saying 'On the Wagon', meaning a person has stopped drinking alcohol originated from a Tyburn tradition. Prisoners were transported to the Gallows on a wagon and were allowed one last drink in a pub on the way to their execution. If offered a second drink by a sympathiser the guard would reply "No, they're going on the wagon!"

Nineteen Eighty-Four (1984)
In the George Orwell novel, Nineteen Eighty-Four (1984) Oranges and Lemons is used as an example of how a shared culture can be eradicated. The nursery rhyme is only partially remembered by the protagonist Winston Smith. Various characters contribute snippets of the rhyme until the verse is completed. But it is lost forever when the final few people who remember it die.

London Bells
- Alternative lyrics to Oranges & Lemons -

. . . .

Gay go up and gay go down
To Ring the Bells of London Town
"Oranges and Lemons" say the Bells of St. Clements
"Bullseyes and Targets" say the Bells of St. Margaret's
"Brickbats and Tiles" say the Bells of St. Giles
"Halfpence and Farthings" say the Bells of St. Martin's
"Pancakes and Fritters" say the Bells of St. Peter's
"Two Sticks and an Apple" say the Bells of Whitechapel
"Maids in white aprons" say the Bells at St. Katherine's
"Pokers and Tongs" say the Bells of St. John's
"Kettles and Pans" say the Bells of St. Anne's
"Old Father Baldpate" say the slow Bells of Aldgate
"You owe me Ten Shillings" say the Bells of St. Helen's
"When will you Pay me?" say the Bells of Old Bailey
"When I grow Rich" say the Bells of Shoreditch
"Pray when will that be?" say the Bells of Stepney
"I do not know" say the Great Bell of Bow
Gay go up and gay go down
To Ring the Bells of London Town.

. . . .

Each of the fifteen Bells of London referred to in the rhyme tell a story about the history, traditions and customs practised in London's bygone days. The words the bells are saying, such as " Oranges and Lemons", "Bullseyes and Targets" and "Pokers and Tongs", reveal the many long gone trades practised and wares sold by the people who lived in the great old city of London. Lord Mayors, Torturers, Executioners and Money Lenders are all obliquely referred to in the words of the bells...

"Oranges and Lemons" say the Bells of St. Clements

St Clements is a small church situated in St. Clements Lane, Eastcheap. There have been three churches on the site starting with the first in the 11th Century when the church is mentioned in a confirmation of grants to Westminster Abbey in 1067. The original old Church was rebuilt in the 15th Century. The second church was destroyed in 1666 during the Great Fire of London. The existing church was rebuilt in 1687 by Sir Christopher Wren (the great architect of St Paul's Cathedral). The Oranges and Lemons refer to the citrus fruits that were unloaded at the nearby docks on the River Thames.

"Bullseyes and Targets" say the Bells of St. Margaret's

St. Margaret's was founded in 1197 but the original church burned down in 1440. It was rebuilt at the expense of Robert Large who was Lord Mayor of London at the time of the disaster. The second church was destroyed in the Great Fire of London of 1666 but rebuilt by Sir Christopher Wren in 1690. The "Bullseyes and Targets" refer to archery which was practised in the nearby fields. In 1363 King Edward III had commanded the obligatory practice of archery on Sundays and holidays. This tradition continued, thus ensuring the safety of the realm, until bows were replaced with guns.

"Brickbats and Tiles" say the Bells of St. Giles

In 1090 a Norman church stood on this site but was rebuilt in 1394 during the reign of King Richard II. The church escaped the Great Fire of London in 1666 but was badly burnt in the Cripplegate Fire of 1897 and was hit by a bomb during World War II. The "Brickbats and Tiles" refers to the bricks and tiles used by nearby builders. The reference to bricks is interesting as bricks were introduced to London by Judge Popham, who resided over the trial of Guy Fawkes immortalised in the Nursery Rhyme Remember, Remember the 5th November.

"Halfpence and Farthings" say the Bells of St. Martin's

St Martin Ongar church, situated in Martin Lane was destroyed in the Great Fire of London in 1666. Only the bell tower, complete with the original bell, has survived in the rectory of St Clements. "You owe me five farthings" relates to the moneylenders who traded nearby.

"Pancakes and Fritters" say the Bells of St. Peter's

St Peter upon Cornhill stands on one of the most historic Christian sites in London. It dates back to AD 179 when it was the site of the Roman basilica built by Lucius, the first Christian ruler of Britain. The name Cornhill derives from the Corn Market which was situated there and dated back to Roman times. The reference to "Pancakes and Fritters" alludes to the wares which were sold to the local workers - the 'fast food' of old London.

"Two Sticks and an Apple" say the Bells of Whitechapel

The bells of Whitechapel do not refer to a church but to the Whitechapel Bell Foundry. The foundry was established in 1570 and was famous for making the Liberty Bell which was shipped to America in 1752 and for making the 'Clock Bells' of St Paul's cathedral in 1709. The Great Clock of Westminster - known as 'Big Ben' is the most famous bell ever cast at Whitechapel. Although the reference to "Two Sticks and an Apple" are not clear, the foundry produced hand bells - similar in shape to toffee apples and this could be the connection. The transport of great bells from the foundry to other parts of London drew great crowds and the atmosphere was similar to that of a fair, where of course toffee apples were traditionally eaten.

"Maids in white aprons" say the Bells at St. Katherine's

The site of St Katherine Cree dates back to 1108 when it was served by the Augustan Priory of Holy Trinity (Christ Church). The church of St Katharine Cree was established as a separate church in the 1200's. It took its name from the original priory as the word 'Cree' is an abbreviation of "Christ Church". The body of the church was rebuilt in 1631 during the years preceding the English Civil War, and is one of only eight churches in the City to survive the Great Fire of London. St Katherine Cree is located near Leadenhall market - so called as it was located, in the 14th century, near a great house which boasted a lead roof. "Maids in white aprons" refers to the costume of the women of the early 1600's who sold their wares in a market near the church.

"Pokers and Tongs" say the Bells of St. John's

The Chapel of St John is the oldest church in London and situated in the Tower of London on the second floor of the White Tower. The Tower of London was built in 1077 - 97 by William the Conqueror. A door from the Great Chamber on the second floor leads to the north aisle of the Chapel of St John the Evangelist. A gruesome discovery was made under the stairs leading to the chapel. The remains of the bodies of the two Little Princes, Edward V and his younger brother Richard, Duke of York were found. They were reputedly killed on the orders of their uncle the Duke of Gloucester, afterwards Richard III (although some scholars name Henry VII as the culprit). The Tower of London was used as a prison for many years and the "Pokers and Tongs" refer to the instruments of torture which were used there!

"Kettles and Pans" say the Bells of St. Anne's

The joint dedication of St Anne's and St Agnes church was mentioned in a grant given by Westminster Abbey in 1467. The original church was devastated during the Great Fire of London in 1666 and was the eleventh church built by Sir Christopher Wren and finished in 1680 (he built 49 churches and the new

St Paul's Cathedral). The church was hit by a bomb during World War II and required extensive reconstruction. The "Kettles and Pans" refer to the utensils sold by the coppersmiths who worked nearby.

"Old Father Baldpate" say the slow Bells of Aldgate
The bells of Aldgate do not refer principally to a church but to the Aldgate Bell foundry. A Master Founder, called Robert Chamberlain, can be traced back through records dated 1420. In 1588 another Master Founder called Robert Mott, who worked for the Aldgate Foundry from 1574 to 1606, recast one of the bells of the Church of St. Botolph's in Aldgate. The Church of St. Botolph's is mentioned in records dating back to 1125. St. Botolph was a pious Saxon Abbot who had built a monastery in Lincolnshire in 654AD. Saint Botolph is the Patron Saint of Boston, Massachusetts. The name was taken as a derivative of "Botolph's town" which became known "Boston". The current church was erected between 1725 and 1740 and dedicated to the Patron Saint of Travellers and Itinerants. The Church of St. Botolph's was known as the 'Prostitute's Church' because the ladies would solicit their trade in this area. Catherine Eddowes, a victim of the notorious Jack the Ripper was seen drunk in the vicinity of the church on the night of her murder on 30th September 1888. Old Father Bald Pate relates to Saint Botolph, a bald pate was a colloquialism used to describe a bald-headed person.

"You owe me Ten Shillings" say the Bells of St. Helen's
A Benedictine nunnery originally formed part of the church which dates back to 1210. In 1538 the nunnery was surrendered to King Henry VIII during the Dissolution of the Monasteries. The convent buildings and land was acquired in 1543 by the Leathersellers' Company. The church was frequented by many rich merchants who lived in the area. These included a Mercer (cloth trader) called Sir John "Rich" Spencer. He became Lord Mayor of London in 1594 during the reign of Queen Elizabeth I. As his nickname indicates he was extremely wealthy as well as being very mean. He also operated as a money lender and explains the reference "You owe me Ten Shillings" in the rhyme. William Shakespeare attended this church (the Bard was also involved in money lending and in 1570 his father John Shakespeare, also a leather seller, was accused in the Exchequer Court of Usury for lending money at the rate of 20% and 25% Interest).

"When will you Pay me?" say the Bells of Old Bailey
The Old Bailey did not have its own bell - it refers to the bells of St. Sepulchre-without-Newgate church and the bell of Newgate prison. St. Sepulchre is the largest church in the City of London and was sited opposite London's courthouse and the infamous Newgate prison which housed both criminals and debtors. The bell of St. Sepulchre marked the time (death

knell) of imminent executions until Newgate prison acquired its own bell. A church has stood on this site since 1137. It was originally called St Edmund-King-and-Martyr but the name was changed during the Crusades to the Church of the Holy Sepulchre. The church was a useful meeting point for the Knights embarking on a crusade as it was positioned just outside the city gate. The church was destroyed by the Great Fire of London and rebuilt by Wren in 1671. The medieval courthouse of London was destroyed in the Great Fire of 1666 and was replaced by London's Central Criminal Court which was used during 1673-1834. The local name for the court was the 'Old Bailey' which was so-called after the street in which it was located (Bailey Street) which was right next to Newgate Prison. The phrase "When will you pay me?" refers to the Debtors housed in Newgate Prison and those tried at the Old Bailey.

"Pray when will that be?" say the Bells of Stepney

St Dunstan's Church is located on Stepney High Street. A church has stood on the site prior to 952 AD, when a stone church was erected, replacing the previous wooden structure. The existing building is the third church to be built on this site and was erected in 1580. There are ten bells in the belfry, dating back to 1385, some which were made at the local Whitechapel Bell Foundry. St Dunstan's has a long traditional link with the sea and it was once known as the 'Church of the High Seas'. Many sailors were buried in the churchyard. The phrase "When will that be?" could possibly refer to wives waiting for sailors to return from voyages with their fortunes, when their 'boat came in'. This was particularly relevant during the 16th and 17th centuries when many sailors were employed on Voyages of Discovery to the New Worlds - their wives would have to wait for their return to receive any wages, but they never knew how long the voyages might be - a two year wait was not uncommon.

"I do not know" says the Great Bell of Bow

St Mary-le-Bow is a historic church in the City of London, off Cheapside. There has been a church on this site dating back to before the arrival of the Normans in 1066. In 1469 the first reference to Bow bells were made in relation to the building of the steeple. In 1631 the poet and Minister John Donne (1572-1631) died and left a bequest for the upkeep of the Bow bell. John Donne wrote the famous poem 'For whom the bell tolls' (No man is an island). The current building was built by Sir Christopher Wren between 1670 and 1680, after the Great Fire of London destroyed the previous church. Dick Whittington, who the famous children's story and pantomime is based on, was a real person (1350 - 1423). He was a Mercer (a dealer in cloth) and was elected Lord Mayor of London four times. In the children's story Dick Whittington leaves London with his cat but is called back by the sound of the ringing of Bow bells.

Cockneys

The Bow bells are important to the traditions of London and it is said that to be a true cockney you must be born within hearing distance of the sound Bow bells. Based on this fact there were no Cockneys born between 11th May 1941 (when the bells were destroyed in a World War II German air raid) and 21st December 1961 (when the Bells rung for the first time after 20 years of restoration work). The BBC used the peal of the bells of Bow at the start of each broadcast to occupied Europe during World War II.

"Here comes a Candle to light you to Bed
Here comes a Chopper to Chop off your Head
Chip chop chip chop - the Last Man's Dead."

The Great Fire of London in 1666

Many of the old London churches were destroyed in the Great Fire of London. The fire started in Pudding Lane in the house and shop of Thomas Farynor who was baker to King Charles II. The King was aware of the risk of fire in baker's shops and ensured that this task was conducted away from the palaces. In the London of 1666 the medieval houses were half timbered, with pitch, and most had thatched roofs - a recipe for disaster in terms of fire risks. The old St Paul's cathedral was destroyed in the fire together with 87 churches. A total of 13,200 houses were also destroyed but amazingly only 6 people were known to have died! Sir Christopher Wren, the great architect, was tasked with the reconstruction of London and built 49 new churches together with the great Cathedral of St. Paul's over a period of 35 years. The city was not subject to re-planning and houses were replaced on exactly the sites of the buildings that were destroyed. To this day the City of London has the same structure which dates back to medieval times. A final note on the Great Fire, the year before, in 1665 the City was decimated by the Great Plague of London which killed 16% of the inhabitants (17,500 out of the population of 93,000) - The Great Fire whilst destroying most of London also purged it of the Plague.

The Chapel of St John is the oldest church in London and situated in the Tower of London.

Made in the USA
Middletown, DE
05 November 2015